Viksit India

Ganesh Natarajan

Urmi Rumi

Qurate
quratebooks.com

Viksit India
Ganesh Natarajan
Urmi Rumi

Published in 2025

© Published by

Qurate Books Pvt. Ltd.
Goa 403523, India
www.quratebooks.com
Tel: 1800-210-6527, Email: info@quratebooks.com

ISBN: 978-93-58983-76-0

Viksit India – The 50 themes

ACKNOWLEDGEMENTS

The idea for this book emerged during a discussion between Ganesh and Urmi after a meeting of entrepreneurs in Pune. In reality, we could not be more different. Ganesh is a busy corporate executive, spending more time on planes than on the ground, and is involved in Boards, consulting, and social ventures. Urmi is a poet, cycling enthusiast, and a deep thinker about people and possibilities.

What we share in common are two things — the joy of writing and the love of our country, not necessarily in that order. Ganesh is the author of fourteen previous books and a thinker and writer on national and global issues. He is also fond of reading prose and poetry and writing limericks. Urmi is a passionate thinker and communicator, has contributed to two previous books and enjoys reading and writing Hindi poetry.

It is this heady mix of English prose and limericks, along with Hindi poetry, that has found expression in this book about India. The idea of "Viksit Bharat," first espoused by Prime Minister Modi and the Government a few years ago, has captured the imagination of many. While some remain skeptical about India becoming a truly developed nation in the foreseeable future, both of us are "dangerous optimists" — we believe that we, as a nation, have what it takes to prove the naysayers wrong and walk the path to truly developed status.

This book offers pointers on how to get there. We thoroughly enjoyed putting these ideas together, with full encouragement from our publisher, Pramod Khera of Qurate. We hope you enjoy the read!

We are grateful to our spouses and daughters for their support and to our publisher, editor and illustrator for their hard word in getting this book done in record time.

Ganesh Natarajan
Urmi Rumi

VISION FOR INDIA

OPENING NOTE
Our Motivation for India

Our Motivation for India

"India is my country; all Indians are my brothers and sisters... I love my country, and I am proud of its rich and varied heritage... In their well-being and prosperity alone lies my happiness." These are the words from the pledge that Urmi, Ganesh, and so many Indians growing up in large and small towns across the country have recited - words meant to instill a sense of patriotism in ourselves and our fellow citizens.

In this day and age, we exult in the many successes we have witnessed and despair at the occasional divisiveness and cynicism—voiced in conversations and, more frequently, on social media. There is much to be proud of in the glorious history and traditions of Bharat, from ancient times through the Hindu, Muslim, and British periods, to the modern post-Independence era of a proud and aspiring Republic of India.

What has always been a source of pride for all of us is the indomitable spirit of our leaders—from Chandragupta Maurya to Chhatrapati Shivaji, from Mahatma Gandhi to Jawaharlal Nehru to Narendra Modi—and our stellar achievements in overcoming larger and more powerful adversaries, whether it was the Mughals or, finally, the British through non-violent resistance and the "Quit India" movement.

In the seventy-five years since Independence, we have managed to preserve the secular fabric of our nation. Today, modern Indians largely do not consider class, caste, or religion when building friendships or professional relationships in organizations.

However, there is still much to be done. There have been occasional fissures in our secular foundation, and although these have reduced in recent years, communal disharmony and caste-based politics have reared their heads on more than one occasion. Economically, productivity in agriculture remains low, and limited employment in the manufacturing sector has led to an over-reliance on services. While we are rightly proud of having climbed to the fourth position in global GDP rankings—and soon to be third—we remain low in terms of GDP per capita and equality of opportunity for all Indians.

Our motivation for India—and for writing this book—is to remind ourselves of our past, our achievements, and the areas that require urgent attention. We also aim to look ahead, exploring the opportunities and imperatives that lie before us in building a truly successful and developed nation.

Our goal is prosperity and happiness for all. To achieve that, we must continue to move onward and upward—until we can proudly call ourselves a *Viksit Bharat*.

Foreword

A developed nation is a dream that many Indians hold close to their hearts and I truly believe we are well placed today to realise this dream and make this a wonderful country to live in for our countrymen. Many of us in India go through struggles in our early years – struggles with indifferent education, weak quality of infrastructure and a growing disparity between the rich and poor. We look forward to the day that urban and rural India will be second to none in the world and every Indian will have the opportunity to live a good life.

It was to realise this dream in small measure for some of India's urban poor that some of us co-founded an entity called Lighthouse Communities Foundation ten years ago. In this decade we have seen tens of thousands of young people enter one of our Lighthouses across sixteen cities and go through a process of connecting with their innate agency, discover their aspirations anew, undertake counselling to choose the right pathway for skills and livelihoods and be worthy citizens of their communities and country. We want to make this dream come true for a million youth by 2030 and we hope many similar institutions will come up that will work in concert with national, state and city Governments, corporations and civil society and make Viksit India a reality for all.

I am glad that Ganesh, my Lighthouse co-founder and Urmi, a young woman with passion and poetry have written this book. May it inspire all of you to strive for success!

Ruchi Mathur

IIM Ahmedabad Batch of 1995
Co-Founder and Vice Chair
Lighthouse Communities Foundation

Contents

SECTION 6 – Entrepreneurship

SECTION 7 – People

SECTION 8 – Love & Inclusion

SECTION 9 – Climate Change

SECTION 10 – Global Bharat

Conclusion:

Section 1

Vision

1.1 The Power to Dream

The agency of a country and all its citizens is realized only when every thinking individual develops the courage and capacity to dream. We observe this in our work in the social sector, where youth from the slums often fail to develop ambition due to a self-imposed belief that their fate (or karma) is to serve and obey others.

No wonder, then, that a young person might attend a skills program in welding, tailoring, or retail—not because they aspire to pursue that profession, but simply to avoid harassment from teachers or relatives urging them to do something "useful" with their lives.

On the other hand, every citizen who believes they can achieve success first develops confidence—and then the power to dream. A positive dream rises above the circumstances of one's birth or upbringing and dares to define new horizons for the future. It defies conventional boundaries and mental barriers, infusing the dreamer with a spirit of "Yes, I can!"

The agenda of Viksit Bharat is not a destination that can be reached by one, a hundred, or even a thousand Indians. It demands an entire generation—crores of young Indians—to develop the power to dream: for their future, their families, their friends, their communities, and indeed, for the nation.

Wise mentors can guide the direction of these dreams and the actions that follow, but they must never subjugate the power to dream—it is the birthright of every citizen of our great country.

So, dream on!

Its real life, not strawberries and cream,
and thoughts that flow in an endless stream.
To think, act and do well,
let's neither wait—nor brood—
let's recreate the power to dream.

It's not just dreams that quietly fade,
nor glimpses of sun from within the shade.
Be it an entrepreneurial gig,
or a career that starts off big—
with millions of dreams, a great nation is made!

एक जुनून बंद नहीं, खुली आँखों का सपना
किसी और का नहीं, बल्कि नितांत ही अपना।

वो युवा बदल देता है अपने और देश के हालात,
जो वाकई चाहता है बढ़ना, लगाता है जज़्बात।

चाहे किसी भी गर्त में गिरा हो वह जन्म से,
एक उन्नत सपना उठा सकता है उसे कर्म से।

सपने देखते रहो, सपनों में बड़ी ताक़त है मेरे भाई,
उन्हीं से प्रेरणा लो फिर तुम्हारी है पूरी खुदाई!

1.2. A Vision for India

India is an idea that has manifested itself in many forms and avatars over the centuries. From the ancient civilization of Bharat to a nation subjugated by centuries of conquest and colonial rule, from a newly independent country to an emerging economic success story — we have witnessed our nation grow stronger, particularly over the past two decades. Today, we can genuinely dream of joining the ranks of developed nations and becoming a leader not just in South Asia, but also in the Global South.

There is much working in India's favor that inspires us to craft a bold and expansive vision for leadership. On the economic front, we are the fastest-growing economy, maintaining control over inflation, our current account deficit, and fiscal deficit, with a low debt-to-GDP ratio and a robust banking and financial services sector. Early strides have been made in our "China plus One" manufacturing strategy, and the stock markets are demonstrating sustained and robust growth, rarely seen elsewhere since the pandemic.

However, this vision of a developed and vibrant India can be jeopardized if disparities persist.

These contradictions were sharply highlighted during a television debate a year ago between two of our most eminent political leaders — Jayant Sinha and Shashi Tharoor. While Jayant emphasized the need for sustainable growth and outlined key pillars to achieve this, Shashi asserted that without true inclusion — where every one of our 1.4 billion citizens believes they have equal opportunities — growth would be hollow and unsustainable. We must, therefore, build a vision for India that is truly inclusive and offers every citizen a fair chance to succeed.

India has been a land of the very poor,
yet some A-raters are going global to conquer.
Will the country be great
for those who dine off a silver plate?
Yes, they will make enormous money, to be sure.

But the true *Bharat* of our dreams
must flourish through multiple streams.
Let's plan for food,
for every Indian and their brood.
Dal-bhat for all — not caviar for the creams!

जो भूखा सोता है मेहनत के बाद
वो क्या सपने देखेगा?
जीवन ही उसका एक दुःस्वप्न
सपने देखने से भी डरेगा

सपने वो देख सकता है
जिसका पेट भरा हो
और जिसका बच्चा, परिवार
दुखों से संकट से न घिरा हो

मेरे इस नए भारत में
सबको सुरक्षा जीवन की
रोज़गार है, संतुष्टि है
नहीं है चिंता भोजन की

शांत मन जो करेगा कल्पना
सुनहरे रुपहले भविष्य की
विकास होगा, नींव सुदृढ़
तकनीक, राजकार्य, समाज की

जब स्वप्नकार समृद्ध हो
नए आयाम छुए जायेंगे
एक दिन हम भारतीय विश्व में
सबसे विकसित कहलायेंगे!

1.3. Vision With Action

How often have we heard in our childhood and youth, *"Stop painting castles in the sky and get up and do some work"?* What is true for individuals is equally true for organizations, communities, and even nations. We keep planning and hoping but often forget to take the robust actions needed to convert our dreams into reality.

Philosopher Joel Barker put it very aptly with an exquisite turn of phrase:

"Vision without action is but a dream.
Action without vision just passes the time.
Vision with action can change the world."

For a country like India, which is determined to transform itself and play a major role in a changing world, *Vision with Action* is the only way forward. Over the past hundred years, we have envisioned many futures and painted numerous pictures of progress. The one vision we did manage to realize through determined action was the attainment of independence. "Swaraj is my birthright" gave rise to a vision of a free India and we embarked on many actions, culminating in our first Prime Minister Nehru's rousing "Tryst with Destiny" speech from the ramparts of the Red Fort.

Today again, we have "promises to keep and miles to go." The immediate goal of becoming the third-largest economy in GDP terms will surely be realized soon, as we already have the momentum. But more challenging goals—for GDP per capita, ensuring every Indian has access to food, education and healthcare—are visions that will require robust and concerted actions.

Let us commit, as a nation, that we will leave no stone unturned on our path to realizing our vision of being *Viksit* by 2047!

"Vision? That's just a dream," they said,
"Get on with the business of earning your bread!"
But do we want to stay the same
with progress that's lame,
or ambition that surges ahead?

"Quit India!" he said—and they agreed to leave,
after silent protests made them believe.
Vision with Action can provide the jolt—
whether for progress or a serious revolt—
let's give the *Viksit* Mission the same big heave!

उठो, जागो और तब तक मत रुको
जब तक लक्ष्य की प्राप्ति न हो जाए
विकास करना हो समझदारी से तो
चौकसी रखो, कोई गलती न हो जाये

प्रगति सिर्फ सपने देखने से नहीं
उनपर सोच विचार के चलने से आती है
बस बेतरतीब अंधाधुंध गोलियां तो
सेनाएं नहीं, आतंकवादी ताकतें चलाती हैं

विकास होगा जब दृढ़ संकल्प हों
दूरदर्शिता, विवेक से काम लेने के
प्रगति की मशाल है, पथ प्रदर्शन हेतु
इस ज्वाला से राख नहीं करना जला के

उत्थान एक मिश्रण हैं दोनों का
उत्साह चाहिए, गंभीरता भी चाहिए
केवल सपनों से नहीं बनती बात
कर्मठता और जूनून भी संग में चाहिए

1.4. Inspiration plus Perspiration

When technology industry doyen Narayan Murthy exhorted Indian youth to work hard—even seventy hours a week—to build the nation, he was met with cheers by a few but jeers by many. The latter believed that work-life balance was the idiom of the times, and that intelligence and innovation alone were enough to build successful careers without the need to pour in long hours of work.

As always, the reality lies somewhere in the middle. Many young individuals have embarked on start-ups and entrepreneurial ventures over the last decade. While a hundred or more have indeed achieved the coveted "unicorn" status—where their businesses crossed a billion dollars in valuation—most others have failed to reach respectable levels of revenue and growth, often abandoning their ventures and returning to employment.

There are many reasons for failure: an inadequately researched idea, a flawed business model, or simply an insufficient market. But quite often, the real reason is that the original inspiration is not followed by adequate perspiration. The path to success is rocky, and it takes hard work to overcome obstacles and move steadily towards one's goals. In any field of human endeavor, it is important to work hard, explore all options, and stay steadfast on the chosen course. Insights and inspiration are vital—but there is no real substitute for hard work.

To end with a quote from poet Henry Wadsworth Longfellow:

"The heights by great men reached and kept were not attained by sudden flight, but they, while their companions slept, were toiling upward in the night."

Too often do we fret , tweet and post
And complain about things we worry about most
The problems we see are all in the mind
The fear of failure can be left behind
Lets try harder, not give up the ghost.

What we need is vision with action
To get outcomes that give us satisfaction
The path to success will be tough
Many an obstacle on a road that is tough
But let make it happen with grit and passion.

प्रेरणा से जगती है आशा
प्रयास करो तो पूरी होती अभिलाषा
सपनों को पंख तभी मिलते हैं
जब पसीना बहता है रास्ते तभी खुलते हैं

सिर्फ़ बुद्धि या कल्पना नहीं है काफ़ी
सफलता के लिए मेहनत में नहीं है माफ़ी
कुछ बनना है तो रातें भी जलानी होंगी
असफलता की चुनौतियाँ अपनानी होंगी

जो थककर रुक जाते हैं राह में,
वो खो देते हैं ऊँचाइयाँ चाह में
प्रेरणा और परिश्रम का सम्मिश्रण
मानव को करना होगा अपना परिश्रम

Section 2

The Idea of India

2.1. Early India

The glorious period of India's history ranges from prehistoric times to the *Gupta dynasty*, encompassing the Indus Valley Civilizations, the Vedic period, and the Mauryan period. This era, locally known as *Prachin Bharat,* witnessed the proliferation of religious diversity, social hierarchies including the caste system, and flourishing art and architecture across the country. Not only did India leave its mark on world history with advances in mathematics, astronomy, and philosophy, but it also laid the foundation for Indian civilization through its traditions, culture, and societal structures.

As we set our sights on an Indian century and make remarkable progress toward a Viksit Bharat, there are many lessons to be learnt from the past.

The traditions of our country may seem wearisome to some—marked by numerous festivals, rituals, and a community of elders within families who wish to uphold these customs without alteration. While there can be no compulsion for future generations to follow these doctrines or practices—as we, the authors, observe significant shifts from our parents to ourselves to our children—India possesses deeply embedded wisdom that we should proudly celebrate and carry forward.

If we were to suggest just three key learnings from ancient India to guide our future, they would be: **respect for family, religious plurality, and relentless youth aspirations.** Among these, the celebration of multiple religions is essential to preserve the diversity and secular nature of our society. Furthermore, enabling youth from all demographic strata to dream freely and helping them find pathways to realize those dreams is a shared responsibility for all of us who envision a *Viksit Bharat.*

Indian heritage is a matter of great pride
for all of us who have swum with the tide
Through the Vedic, Maurya, and Gupta time
a country that was once at its very prime
is now ready for the next big *Viksit* ride!

The love for our country has always run deep
And the road ahead is rugged and steep
But our glorious culture and heritage
Will surely place us on that world stage
Let's tighten our belts for the next big leap!

वेदों का देश, ये है पुराणों का देश
स्वर्ण और रजत, कीर्तिमानों का देश

विश्वगुरु यूँ ही नहीं पड़ा इसका नाम
सभ्य और संपन्न, प्रकृति से अभिराम

संस्कृति के संस्कारों की यह जन्मस्थली
सुलझ गयी सरलता से मानवीय प्रश्नावली

विकसित ही था, लगा असमय अल्पविराम
अब फिर से जगा है अंतस में कोहराम

फिर से विश्व का गुरु बन दिखलाना है
विकास के परचम नभ पर फहराना है

रास्ता लम्बा है असंभव उसको क्या है,
जिसने सदियों समय के बहाव को सहा है

जिसकी आदिकाल से जीत से ही प्रीत है
उस भारत को ज्ञात है चुनौतियां ही रीत हैं

2.2. The Mughal Rule

The fortunes of India changed with the rise of six major Mughal emperors who ruled over the subcontinent from the sixteenth to the nineteenth century. Many of us, having studied history in Indian schools, are more familiar with the Mughal Empire than with the ancient Indian dynasties that preceded it or the British rule and independent India that followed.

What characterized the Mughal Empire, and what can we learn from that era to help pave the way for a *Viksit Bharat*?

The first, and unfortunate, reality was that of dynastic rule. From Babur to Humayun, to the great Emperor Akbar, and then Jahangir, Shah Jahan, and the despotic Aurangzeb, the emperors were diverse in their personalities, yet each ascended the throne by virtue of lineage. While meritocracy may have prevailed among the masses during Akbar's reign, there was no denying that the Supreme Leader was always the Azeem-o-Shaan Shehenshah This dynastic culture is still visible in some political groups in our country today. Unlike the more evolved governments of Europe and the United States, we remain prone to electing or selecting the sons and daughters of our leaders to inherit positions of power and authority.

However, a positive aspect of Mughal rule was their tolerance of other religions and their willingness to appoint many Hindus to high positions in both the military and administration. There is much to learn from both the successes and failures of the empire. If we are to build a truly developed nation, we must study that period with sincere interest.

IIf the Taj Mahal is a tribute to love,
There's the spirit of both wolf and dove
In the rule of the Mughals, mighty and bold,
With trumpets and bugles, their stories unfold
Lessons lie on earth and in the skies above.

The mighty kings—Babur, Humayun, and Akbar
In times when lions would roar and kittens purr
Taught us lessons of friendship and grace,
To let hatred burn without a trace,
In the nation we dream to build and treasure.

सच है ये, मानव सीखता है इतिहास से
दिव्य भविष्य बनता है स्वर्णिम अतीत से

मुग़लिया तहज़ीब और अदब की मज़बूती
संगेमरमर सी सफ़ेदी, प्राणों की आहुति

सिर्फ "मारो लूटो छीनो" वाली हरकत नहीं
परंपरा मंगोल, ईरानियों, यूनानियों सी नहीं

तोड़ा नहीं, इस ज़मीन को अपना घर बनाया
मुग़ल ताज ने इसे बड़ी मोहब्बत से बसाया

सीखने को बहुत, काफ़ी अपनाया जा चुका
दोस्ती और अमन का परचम फहराया जा चुका

अब पाठ जो सीखे हुए, फिर दोहराने होंगे
भारत के भविष्य की नींव में चुनवाने होंगे

2.3. The English Rule

Most of us have some experience or inherited memory of the British Raj in India, which ended only at the dawn of independence. Ganesh's own grandfather, who moved from a village in Kerala to the city of Bombay in 1929, began working for a Western company. Over time, he transitioned from traditional Indian attire to impeccable English wear and distinguished himself in his career through unwavering loyalty to his Western employers.

On the other hand, many recall the early, fragmented—but eventually powerful—days of the Quit India Movement. Movements led by figures like Subhash Chandra Bose and Mahatma Gandhi have now become part of India's glorious history as the nation marched toward its famous "tryst with destiny."

Some speak fondly of the British Raj, while many utterly detest the thought of having been subjugated for so many years by foreign rulers. Yet there is no denying that several pillars of modern India, including the railways, were established during that period. The fact that many of us studied in English convents, and that urban Indians are often as comfortable with English as with their native languages, has undoubtedly contributed to the global success of Indians in the Western world.

Like it or hate it, the English period in India—like the Mughal period before it—undeniably lcft its mark on the country.

Viksit India

There was a time when India was in a daze,
Overawed by the glamour of the Angrez.
For our ancestors in towns and villages,
It wasn't fear of loot and pillages,
But the allure of the Sahib that would amaze.

The struggle for freedom took many a decade,
as our brothers endured many a punishment and raid.
With the valour of Patel, Nehru, and Gandhi,
We marched through the Quit India *aandhi,*
and a proud nation finally stepped out of the shade.

हर पल की हर घटना का होता है कुछ परिणाम
भारत पर अंग्रेजी शासन के ये हैं कुछ आयाम

हिन्दुस्तान सोने की चिड़िया, जाना माना नाम
इसी लालच से अंग्रेज़ आये थे, लूटी समृद्धि तमाम

लेकिन इसके बस एकमुखी ही नहीं थे अंजाम
चमक अंग्रेजी हुकूमत की थी, करते थे सब सलाम

नकली सुख था, कितने दिन चलता ये लूटपाट का काम
अब अंग्रेज़ों से हुए बेचैन सभी, मचने लगा कोहराम

मुक्त होना था, लगी 'साहिब' होने के जूनून पर लगाम
सेवा की स्वतंत्रता सेनानियों ने, भक्ति की निष्काम

भागे अंग्रेज़ देश से, भारतियों के जज़्बे को प्रणाम
भारत माता का परचम लहराया हासिल हुआ मुकाम

2.4. Gandhi and Quit India

The stories of Mahatma Gandhi and his approach through *Ahimsa* (non-violence), civil disobedience, and the Quit India movement to drive the British out of India have been a standard part of every Indian child's education. There were many approaches taken in the fight for independence — notably those of Bhagat Singh and Subhas Chandra Bose — but it was the steady and unbending will of Gandhi, supported by great leaders of the era including Sardar Vallabhbhai Patel and Pandit Jawaharlal Nehru, that finally prevailed over the British.

There are many inspiring stories about Mohandas Karamchand Gandhi that we all remember — from his early humiliation on a train in South Africa to his simple life at the Sabarmati Ashram; from the numerous tours and fasts he undertook to unite the nation against a common foe, to the sheer will he displayed both in India and abroad to secure India's status as a proud, independent nation.

History is full of world figures — from the kings of England to towering political leaders like Abraham Lincoln, Mao Tse Tung, and more recently, Nelson Mandela — but the legacy of Gandhi will always remain dear to all of us in India, and indeed, to peaceful people all over the world. Gandhi was truly a *Mahatma* — a great soul — in our country and in our midst.

Ours is a land that has known many leaders,
from the early days of saints and healers.
We watched and heard of Ashoka the Great,
and stories of Shivaji we love to narrate —
but one name shines bright for all readers.

He came back from Africa, Gujarat-born and bred,
a man of great compassion, thoughtful and well-read.
Gandhi, the sage with a vision so clear,
Helped India break free, casting off fear
and led us to progress, with hope widespread.

कौन नहीं जानता बापू को!

हर हिंदुस्तानी की रगों में बापू की सीख बहती है
हिंदुस्तान के हर प्रतीक चिन्ह में बापू की आत्मा रहती है

कैसे कोई शांत बैठ भी कर देता है क्रांति
बिना हाथ उठाये भी कैसे मिलती है आज़ादी

विश्व में शायद ही कोई ऐसा जादू कर पाया
पूरे जनमानस को जिसने एक कर के दिखलाया

सम्प्रेषण ही शक्ति है, गुरुमंत्र दे कर चले गए
मोहनदास करमचंद से बापू होकर अमर हुए

सत्याग्रह नाम का कैवल्य, भारत के सपूतों के नाम
और नहीं कोई, बस बापू ही कर सकते थे ये काम

अद्भुत व्यक्तित्व ने सबको कर दिया सम्मोहित, मंत्रमुग्ध
देश के स्वतंत्रता आंदोलन में आहूति थी ये सबसे शुद्ध!

2.5. Tourist Destination

One campaign that truly captured the imagination of citizens, both in India and abroad, was the tourism tagline coined by visionary bureaucrat Amitabh Kant. *"Incredible India"* became the watchword for Indian embassies worldwide. As a result, both overseas and domestic visitors began frequenting not just well-known destinations like the Taj Mahal, Jaipur, and Kerala, but also embarked on backpacking tours through India's rich history and culture.

For passionate global travelers, India presents a veritable kaleidoscope of colors, aromas, and experiences. Many of our friends from the US, Europe, and the Middle East have visited India not just once, but multiple times. However, for a variety of subtle and obvious reasons, India's ability to consistently attract new tourists has fallen short. Americans, Europeans, and even travelers from Latin America and Southeast Asia tend to stick to familiar and favorite destinations, often giving the Indian experience a miss.

A critical aspect of a *Viksit Bharat* will be the tripling—or even quadrupling—of tourist inflows over the next two decades. Achieving this will require action on three key fronts – creating excitement through immersive audio-visual and virtual reality experiences in key cities, while ensuring safety, promoting multiple destinations to encourage visits to a variety of destinations for first-time and repeat visitors and practicing "Atithi Devo Bhava" with well-educated and courteous tourist guides, high security and efficient transport systems, and responsive government mechanisms.

Let us take pride in our India and open her doors to the world with warmth and confidence.

Our India, we believe, is truly incredible,
but how do we get the tourists to double?
Let's open our doors,
Show the grandeur of our shores,
and make every journey unforgettable!

Time to polish the antique silverware,
Twirl the moustaches of sentries with flair,
Flash our best smile,
Even if they stay awhile,
and unleash the shopping till our cupboards are bare!

सुन्दर है आपका देश, पर सुरक्षा कहाँ है?
जिसमें सकुशल रह पाए हमारा नागरिक
पर्यटक के लिए वैसा नक्शा कहाँ है?

विश्व ने माना हमारी सुन्दर धरा का स्थान
लेकिन खुद के बन्दों की दुर्दशा देख,
उनके विरुद्ध होते जुर्म को देख हुए परेशान

भारत देश के लिए ये ज़रूरी होगा
कि इस विहंगम भूभाग को कर दें सुगम भी
इसे स्वच्छ बनाना भी लाज़मी होगा

क्यों न विकसित होने की डगर चलते
पर्यटन के लिए नए रास्ते और आयाम बना,
क्यों नहीं हम बेहतर के हेतु बदलते

इतना समृद्ध फिर हमारा वातावरण हो
सभी को आमंत्रित करे, सभी को लुभाये,
हमारा आतिथ्य सत्कार एक उदहारण हो !

Section 3

Infrastructure

3.1 Roads and Bridges

One of the greatest sources of pride for India over the past twenty years has been the development of the country's surface transport infrastructure. From the days soon after independence—when Indians could only hum the famous song *"Country Roads, take me home"*—to the launch of the Golden Quadrilateral Project, and more recently, the National Highways Development Project, the Bharatmala Pariyojana, and the construction and upgrading of bridges under the Setu Bharatam Mission, progress has been sure and speedy in all respects.

The success of the United States initially, and later China, can largely be attributed to their exceptional road connectivity. For many decades, Indian exporters were hampered by the lack of reliable and efficient road networks. However, the recent development of national highways, toll expressways, and state and district roads has substantially addressed that shortcoming. The country now also boasts of impressive bridges—most notably the Chenab Bridge, whose deck stands 322 metres above the Chenab River, making it the world's tallest railway bridge.

Reversing the trend of excessive urban crowding, facilitating the transportation of goods within the country and to ports for export, and enabling the mobility of people within cities and across states—these are the most reliable indicators of progress. We must also remember that the truest sign of development is not when the poor start buying cars, but when the rich begin using public transport. While we still have a long way to go, the progress in recent years has been remarkable, and we must continue to accelerate on this path forward.

Suhana safar hai aur yeh mausam haseen,
Humein dar hai hum kho na jaayein kahin.
In India, it may not be just weather,
But with bad roads, the question was whether
The traveler would reach or be lost in a ravine.

Reaching in two hours on the Mumbai-Pune expressway,
Or traveling high over the Chenab on a sunny day,
India's new roads and bridges
Are no longer just pathways and hedges—
With great infrastructure, we are now up, up, and away.

जीवन चलने का ही नाम
चलते रहना प्रवृत्ति मनुष्य की
लेकिन राह ही ना मिले तो
क्या दशा हो जनमानस की

देश विशाल, सुदूर ग्राम हैं
सबको जोड़ना धर्म बने
तभी होगा सामान विकास
तभी प्रगति की बात बने

कैसे पहुंचेगा फायदा सब तक
जो न हो कोई दृढ़ साधन
गड्ढों में फंस जायेगा मामला
नहीं कर पायेगा काम प्रशासन

अब ऐसे हैं हालात सब तरफ
सड़क ने सबकुछ जोड़ा है
दशरथ मांझी न बने अब कोई
सरकार ने मजबूरी को तोड़ा है

3.2 Trains and Planes

Walk into any new train station or airport in India these days, and you're immediately struck by the elegance of design and the world-class conveniences and technologies. The quality of new train systems like Vande Bharat, along with older but reliable ones like the *Rajdhani, Geetanjali,* and *Shatabdi Expresses*, has brought joy back to train travel in the country.

Air travel, too, has become far more pleasant, with multiple airline options and the speed at which one can pass through airports—thanks to services like Digi Yatra and Fast Forward—making a significant difference. Combined with the remarkably efficient immigration processes at most large airports, both domestic and international travel now offer a level of ease and comfort often equal to, and sometimes surpassing, the best that the West or Southeast Asia has to offer.

Elsewhere in this book, we've discussed the need for India to greatly accelerate both domestic and international tourism. One of the major impediments in the past—the inconvenience of travel into and within the country—has now been substantially addressed. While airline quality still leaves something to be desired, the growing competition to market leader IndiGo, particularly from a rejuvenated Air India, offers hope that reliability and passenger comfort will improve in the not-too-distant future.

A proud and developed nation must provide easy, comfortable travel for its citizens—and India has come a long way in this regard. Full credit goes to the Government for enabling such rapid improvements. We look forward to even more innovations and better journeys in the decade ahead.

Travel in India was always edgy,
With packed stations and crowds going crazy.
But today's super trains and stations,
Leave no cause for palpitations,
And in airports, just whiz through with Digi!

You don't have to be an astronaut like Suni,
Just a traveler who doesn't want to go loony,
and as more and more of us get up and go,
the travel horrors seem an era ago.
On a great future for transport, let's put our money!

चलो, गिरो, उड़ो – बस रुको मत!
ये बातें तो सब ज्ञानी कहते हैं
कैसे कोई बढ़ेगा आगे दोस्त
यान ही अगर खस्ताहाल रहते हैं

क्या अंग्रेज़ों ने सोचा था तब
भारत रेल बनेगी इतनी विशाल?
राइट बंधुओं ने किया होगा विचार
कि प्रगतिशील देश करेगा कमाल?

बाप दादाओं ने खाये धक्के
धीमी थी विकास की गति
विश्वस्तर का हुआ बदलाव
दिखने लगी इस क्षेत्र में प्रगति

प्रगति के नए आयाम को
छूने लगा है भारत देश
रेल कहो या बोलो वायुमार्ग
बढ़त दिखी है बहुत विशेष

अब देखेंगे कैसे रूकती है
गाड़ी हमारी चलती तेज़
पूरी दुनिया अब पहुँच में
विकसित भारत हैरत अंगेज़

3.3 Logistics Hub

Seven engines of growth are firing on all cylinders in India to make **superior logistics** the focus of future economic development. Roads, ports, airports, railways, waterways, mass transport, and logistics infrastructure are the key pillars of the **PM Gati Shakti National Master Plan.** In addition, an integrated multi-modal logistics hub spanning **900 acres in Northern India,** along with a digital platform that integrates key logistics processes under the **Unified Logistics Interface Platform (ULIP),** will work together to make Indian goods more competitive, promote sustainable practices, and create large-scale employment opportunities in the Indian logistics sector.

Logistics is one area where India's progress as a nation—and particularly our manufacturing competitiveness—has long lagged behind. For a significant period, it was cheaper to buy New Zealand apples in Mumbai than apples from Himachal Pradesh, due to the poor state of cold chain transportation. The substandard quality of roads, especially those off the main highways, significantly slowed down traffic, leading to delays in reaching ports and further delays in stuffing and loading containers.

Logistics and multi-modal supply chains required more holistic thinking and substantial investments in the entire ecosystem of production, warehousing, land transportation, and shipping. This has been the Government's focus over the past few years—and the results are now becoming visible. The use of digital tools and AI to predict weak points in the supply chain, across state and national boundaries, has proven to be a valuable asset in optimizing the flow of goods and information.

India is well poised to replicate what Singapore has achieved—on a much larger scale. We **can and must** become a global logistics hub and ensure that every manufacturer and exporter, in every part of the country, has access to world-class logistics facilities that deliver goods **better, faster, and cheaper** into the hands of customers.

Every global economy needs excellent design.
End to end supply chains and transportation divine
From warehouse to shop floor,
Goods have to flow to every door,
with efficiency and costs in line.

Roads with potholes are becoming highways of glass
India' s infrastructure is now truly world class
So will the goods we make
give all competition a shake?
Yes our supremacy shall come to pass!

विकसित भारत हैरतअंगेज़सड़कों से रेलों तक, हर मार्ग अब सुगम हुआ
गति शक्ति की योजना से, भारत का सपना सच हुआ

मल्टी-मोडल हब में, समाहित है नव विचार,
डिजिटल प्लेटफॉर्म से मिल, हर प्रक्रिया पारदर्शी और स्पष्ट व्यवहार

गोदाम से बंदरगाह तक, सफर हुआ है आसान,
एआई और तकनीक ने दी सप्लाई चेन को नई पहचान

चमकती हैं सड़कें, तेज़ हैं जलमार्गों की धार,
हर निर्माता को मिलता, वैश्विक व्यापार का उपहार

प्रतिस्पर्धा में अग्रणी, भारत का बढ़ता मान,
लॉजिस्टिक्स में उत्कृष्टता से, बनेगा देश महान।

3.4 Digital India

It was the visionary Prime Minister of India, Atal Bihari Vajpayee, who once said, "IT is India's Tomorrow." He might not have imagined just how profoundly digital technology would influence every aspect of India's life and work in the following two decades. Much of this progress can be attributed to two successive governments, which inducted Nandan Nilekani at the Union Cabinet level to establish the UIDAI, with the mandate of providing a unique identity to every citizen of India.

The progress under the Modi Government has been truly praiseworthy. From the success of the JAM trinity (Jan Dhan, Aadhaar, and Mobile) to the proliferation of BharatNet and the National Optical Fibre Network, it has become possible for nearly all Indians to enjoy a unique digital identity, receive direct benefit transfers to their Jan Dhan accounts, and make transactions through a ubiquitous mobile app-based payment network. From an era in which, as a Harvard professor once remarked, "Half of India is waiting for a telephone, and the rest are waiting for a dial tone," the transformation to a Digital India has been both an evolution and a revolution.

Where can Digital India take us on the pathway to a truly *Viksit Bharat* (Developed India)? Today, it is already transforming the lives of millions. Recent innovations like DigiYatra are accelerating travel and providing numerous benefits that simplify daily life. In the years ahead, continued investments in digital infrastructure—along with ambitious initiatives like the ₹10,000 crore National AI Mission—will unlock new opportunities for businesses and entrepreneurs, building robust pathways to a successful future.

They said it couldn't be done,
a nation of mystics the world would shun.
But we built a nation of tech,
with many hands on deck,
and in doing so, had a ton of fun.

A 200 billion industry we may be now,
but with AI and products, we need to figure how.
We can be two trillion,
and employ many a million,
to make the world sit up and say, "Wow!"

पैसा ही तो जीवन है
प्यार से पेट भरता नहीं
ये बात तार्किक है
कवियों को ये पटेगी नहीं

राउंड फिगर कर दो भाई
ठीक है, लेकिन खुल्ला दो
काली कमाई हर जगह लुटाई
चेंज नहीं है टॉफी ले लो

एक फ़ोन में समा गया
रूपए पैसों का पूरा संसार
ऑनलाइन पेमेंट्स ने ही
कितना कम कर दिया भ्रष्टाचार

गाँव शहर में अब भी लेकिन
नहीं है पूरी समानता
आगे होगा ये अब कि
फैलेगी डिजिटल साक्षरता

हर भारतीय अब बनेगा
डिजिटल इंडियन सम्पूर्ण
भविष्य होगा सशक्त सुदृढ़
तकनीक से होगा हर सिस्टम परिपूर्ण

3.5 UPI for the World

The Unified Payments Interface (UPI) has been the poster child of Digital India, transforming the payments system within the country and increasingly gaining traction in different parts of the world. A brainchild of tech industry icon Nandan Nilekani, UPI offers a unique combination of real-time fund transfers, interoperability across various payment platforms and banks, and high security through virtual payment addresses.

The convenience of being primarily mobile-based and the widespread use of QR codes have made it remarkably user-friendly at merchant platforms across India. Today, from significant commercial transactions to a small donation made to a cow bearing a QR code on its back in the holy city of Varanasi, UPI has become truly ubiquitous.

The logical next step for UPI is its extension to international travelers in India and Indians abroad, as well as establishing UPI as a key global payment switch. India has already partnered with nations like Bhutan and the tech-savvy Singapore. As is well known, the power of a network multiplies as more nodes are added.

By the time India achieves its goal of becoming a developed nation (Viksit Bharat), it is expected that most countries in the Global South will be enthusiastic adopters of UPI. With more European and American nations following Singapore's lead, a global, friction-free payment web can be established.

Of course, challenges remain—KYC (Know Your Customer) requirements must be addressed for each jurisdiction, cross-border transaction fees and credit card exchange rate markups need to be navigated, and greater global awareness of the UPI One World service must be cultivated. Yet, the end goal will undoubtedly be worth the effort.

Whether in a busy street or on a golf course
There could be a situation no worse
To have no cash
To pay for a small bash
But UPI leaves no reason for remorse.

With JanDhan Aadhar and Mobility done
The fun with Digital had just begun
And now when we just whip
our phones to pay for a chip
And get on with our busy lives to run!

सिक्के, नोट लिए फिरते थे
जेब भारी हो तो ही
सपने पूरे कर पाते थे

धीरे धीरे बदला दौर
प्लास्टिक मनी का ट्रेंड आया
धन एक टुकड़े में समाया
बटुए में सब कुछ समाया

फिर आयी एक नयी लहर
हर एक के हाथ में स्मार्टफोन आया
डिजिटल पैसों का ये दौर
तेज़ी से आदत में समाया

अब फ़ोन के एक टैप से
लेन देन मुमकिन हुआ है
देश के विकास का द्योतक
भारतवासी स्मार्ट बना है!

Section 4

Growth Sectors

4.1 Make in India

IIn an earlier book titled "Pathways to India's Success", co-edited by Ganesh Natarajan, there was a commentary on the decline of manufacturing as a percentage of Indian GDP and the need to focus on three key areas in the future:

Areas like rare earths, where there is a huge asymmetry with advanced manufacturing nations like China,

Sectors like pharmaceuticals, where domestic demand—and eventually global demand—can be met through a combination of Atmanirbhar (self-reliance) and Atmavishwas (self-confidence),

Global industry-building opportunities such as consumer electronics and microprocessors.

As a nation, we have taken stock of our lacunae and identified key focus areas, including innovation, skill development, IP protection, and investment facilitation. Several major initiatives have been launched, such as the Manufacturing PLI schemes, PM Gati Shakti and overall infrastructure improvement. Early results have been encouraging, with over **$600 billion in investments over the last ten years.**

If a Viksit Bharat (Developed India) can establish a mega manufacturing base that balances automation with manual labour and ensures significant value addition within the country, a major part of our national dream would be realized. While India has done a superb job in services and has established itself as one of the top technology providers in the world, the **real goal**—in terms of both economic growth and employment generation—lies in manufacturing. Onward !

It's the age-old representation of the family man.
The blue collared worker back home in the factory van
It was the sweat on his brow.
And the hard-working furrow
That encouraged him through his life span.

Make in India in future will have a different flavour
With traditional manual labour out of favour
CNCs. Automation, Flexible Manufacturing Systems
With the human at the centre with several automation items
Putting manufacturing back as a career to adore!

याद तो है न? कुछ ही सौ तो साल हुए हैं
पूरे विश्व में भारत के माल – सामानों के चर्चे हुए हैं

इतना था कमाल का उत्पादन कि गोरे चकित थे
अपनी नावों में बैठ बैठ, भारत को ढूंढने निकले थे

देखा गया भारतवर्ष में तकनीक और संस्कृति का मेल
विकास की मानसिकता, जैसे बाएं हाथ का खेल

इस धरती को अब फिर से, इस तरफ ध्यान देना होगा
बने यहीं हर चीज़ काम की, इसे क्रांति बनाना होगा

यहीं बनाओ, यहीं बनेगा – जो ठान लें हम सब
अपना भारत बढ़ेगा तेज़ी से, जग देखेगा एकटक

4.2 IT Services

Dewang Mehta, arguably the first true evangelist for IT services from India, had a favourite joke in the nineties.

An Arab Sheikh dies in the desert. When the Bedouins gather around, they discover his will, which says, "Give half my camels to my first son, one-third to my second son, and one-ninth to my last son." They round up the camels and find seventeen. Unable to divide them as instructed, they send a fax to NASSCOM in India. A month later, a young Ganesh Mehta arrives at their camp riding his camel. After understanding the problem, he says, "Just keep my camel." Now there are eighteen camels. The first son gets nine, the second gets six, and the third gets two.

"Hey, there's one camel left!" says the new chief.

"That's my camel," says Ganesh, and rides off into the sunset!

This joke, which we repeated across countries and continents, truly captured the power of India's IT services industry—not merely "body shopping" or staffing, as cynics would claim, but Indian intelligence and innovation unleashed on computational problems worldwide. Over the decades, the industry has scaled new heights—from offshore outsourcing to product engineering, from digital transformation to the rise of Global Capability Centers spreading across the country.

What does the future hold? The landmark of $300 billion is within reach. Once the current growth pause is overcome, the industry is expected to harness AI and automation to deliver innovative solutions across the board to global clients. There will be new peaks to conquer and fresh opportunities to unveil, but this is one industry that refuses to rest on its laurels. The climb to the summit continues.

The clouds persist, both cirrus and cumulus
As Indian companies try to board the new AI bus.
For software services, growth was in plenty.
If not thirty percent, at least twenty
and it's our talent that was always the plus.

For every Ram Rahim and software Joe
The past few months have seen some woe.
All of us who have been here for years.
Are open to opportunity, with eyes and ears.
So that the industry finds a new mojo!

वो दिन भी क्या दिन थे!

सवालों को नए तरीकों से हल कर रही थी
भारतीय तकनीक बुलंदियां छू रही थी
रचनात्मक निदान अभियंता चुटकियों में ले आते
और दिमाग का लोहा दुनिया मान रही थी

सिर्फ कर्मचारी बनाकर नहीं ले जाना चाहते थे
वे तो हमारे इंजिनीर्स के कर्मयोग को पूज रहे थे
कहीं उलझनों से पूरी पूरी टीमें उलझ रही थीं
तो कहीं चुटकियों में हम मुश्किलें सुलझा रहे थे

फिर वक़्त बदला, तकनीकों में तहलका मच गया
कृत्रिम का ज़माना आया, इंसान पीछे रह गया
अब आगे बढ़ना हो तो क्या करेंगे, कुछ ठीक नहीं
संसार में दिमागी कमाल का दाम गिर गया

देर नहीं हुई है, बस अपना रवैया बदलना होगा
नयी नयी बातों हैं, उनकी तह में गोता लगाना होगा
सीखना सिखाना होगा उच्च स्तर पर नवाचार
हमें इन मशीनों से बहुत आगे बढ़ना होगा

4.3 IT Products

Many naysayers of India's technology success ask, "But where are the world-beating software products? Why hasn't a single SAP, Facebook, ChatGPT, or DeepSeek emerged from India? How long will we continue to deploy our brightest minds merely to manage someone else's network, test their software, or write code for products built in India but branded and sold as Western innovations?"

Beyond this lament lies a harsh reality: barring the occasional successes like Zoho or Fresh works, India lacks a robust ecosystem and sufficient marketing investment to support Deep Tech, products, and platforms. As Atul Batra, product evangelist and community leader of NASSCOM's Tech community, aptly says, "Unless India's domestic market consumption grows considerably from the current paltry level; we will remain a shallow tech nation. It needs to be incentivized!"

The future must see a healthy mix of both products and services, all proudly carrying the "Made in and Delivered from India" tag. Becoming a leading nation in products, startups, and innovation is a worthy aspiration—but it requires strong focus on five critical factors: Talent acceleration,a thriving domestic market for products, Patient capital to encourage breakthrough innovations, world-class academia engaged in R&D, and expansion of the tech ecosystem to at least 25 cities across India.

As we progress towards becoming a *Viksit Bharat* (Developed India), the technology product industry must aim to generate at least $100 billion entirely from within the country. This may not seem overly ambitious, but it can serve as a solid milestone toward the greater dream of placing India among the top three most innovative nations in the world.

How good is your software industry, they said.
We do great in services, which every youth wants to tread.
In every team and each abode
There is a young person writing code.
But in the product and innovation area, we are deep in the red!

Talent and spirit, we have in a large dose.
Our industry is exciting but only when it grows.
What we need is innovation and research.
To get deep tech and products to truly surge
And get the furrow off the cynic's brows!

कोड लिखे हैं वर्षों से, क्या हम बस सेवा करें
अब बारी है भारत की, अपनी भी परवाह करें

ज़ोहो, फ्रेशवर्क्स की तरह, और सितारे हों,
'Made in India' के तले, अपने गुज़ारे हों।

सेवा से उत्पाद तक, बढ़े कदम ये ठोस,
पर जो खरीदे न कोई, कहाँ रहेगा जोश?

शिक्षा, कौशल, पूंजी भी, नवाचार हो जाए
रिसर्च में हो दीप जलें, फैले विज्ञान की राहें

पच्चीस शहरों में गूंजे, टेक्नोलॉजी का राग,
संभावनाओं के देश में, क्यों हो सपनों का अभाव?

सौ अरब की राह नहीं, कोई बहुत बड़ी बात,
आज कर दिखाएं कुछ बढ़िया, हो जाये अमृतपात

4.4 Agriculture

Agriculture, while continuing to provide the largest number of direct and indirect jobs in the Indian economy, has been a story of many missed opportunities and now accounts for just 16 percent of India's GDP. However, on an aggregate basis, an India rank second in farm output worldwide and is a global leader in the production of fruits and vegetables, spices, and holds a high market share in rice, wheat, dairy, and meat products.

The government has had its share of major successes, like the Green Revolution, which significantly increased food production and reduced dependence on imports, along with some setbacks, such as the failed introduction of the farm bills. Many challenges persist, including low farm productivity and weak water management, with several areas overly dependent on the monsoon.

However, there is notable progress in new opportunity areas. Sustainable agricultural practices and innovative approaches like agroforestry, aquaculture, organic farming, and hydroponic farming are gaining traction. Technological adoption—through widespread drone usage and farm mechanization—is poised to become a key enabler, enhancing future agricultural efficiency and productivity.

As we move forward, if we can encourage both men and women to willingly take responsibility for the growth and betterment of farms—and ensure that children are kept out of farms and village markets and instead enrolled in schools—we can look forward to an India where industry and agriculture exist as balanced pillars of a vibrant economy.

A good day for Hari at his farm,
No worry about crops and no animal harm.
At times, it's a place where all is well,
giving the family food to dwell,
and keeping them safe, content, and warm.

Agriculture must be a major drive
for a nation where farmers must strive.
In a land where over fifty percent
seek a life that's decent and content,
we must help every rural soul to thrive.

हर किसान के खेत में आई बहार,
ना चिंता अब, ना कोई उधार
सफेद दूध, हरी सब्ज़ी आये,
हर थाली में रोटियाँ मुस्काए

गायें मस्त, बछड़े नाचें,
धूप में गेहूँ की बालियाँ साजें।
संध्या को जब घर लौटे किसान,
चेहरे पर न हो सुकून, न कि थकान

कृषि बने अब गर्व की बात,
हर किसान के अच्छे हों हालात
सौ में पचास जो खेती में लगे
उनके सपने सच क्यों न बनें?

नई मशीन, बीज हो नया,
हो सुरक्षा भरा सरकार का साया
जब गांव खिले, तब देश खिले,
हर खेत से अमृत-धारें मिलें।

4.5 Healthcare

Healthcare in India presents both a massive challenge—given the country's scale and complexity—and a tremendous opportunity to offer low-cost, high-quality medical and hospital care to the world. Our primary healthcare systems remain weak, and the quality of hospitals ranges widely—from world-class, commercial private institutions to a few exemplary government-run centers like AIIMS and JIPMER.

A significant rural-urban divide persists, with poor healthcare infrastructure and outcomes in many rural areas, especially in the aspirational districts. Inadequate insurance coverage further limits access to high-quality, high-cost healthcare services, leaving many Indians underserved. Clearly, much needs to be done to improve domestic healthcare outcomes.

The Government has launched several important initiatives. Ayushman Bharat aims to provide health insurance coverage to 100 million of the most vulnerable families. Additionally, the National Health Policy and Digital Health Mission are focused on enabling electronic health records, expanding telemedicine services, and achieving universal health coverage and access for all.

This is not to say that developed countries like those in Europe or the U.S. have it all figured out—while access may be better, costs are frequently exorbitant. India has already become a hub for medical tourism, with hospitals in cities like Mumbai, Pune, and Hyderabad offering surgical packages that include post-procedure vacations for patients and their families. However, this sector remains underexploited and has significant potential for growth.

Healthcare is undoubtedly a key sector to watch over the next decade and beyond.

When we had a cough or a sneeze,
the family doctor put us at ease.
But now, with steep fees and endless delays,
we avoid hospitals for as long as it stays—
Getting treated is torture, not a breeze!

Ayushman Bharat's a noble aim,
to give every citizen a fairer game.
To stay well and thrive,
mass joy we can derive
Let's bring this mission to national fame!

भीड़-भाड़ में उलझा भारत,
स्वास्थ्य बना हुआ है संकट
गाँवों में अब भी दर्द पुराना,
शहरों में सुविधा, गाँव इस से अनजाना

AIIMS, JIPMER जैसे सितारे,
पर सुदूर कोनों में अब भी अंधियारे
बिना बीमा के टूटे हैं सपने,
बिन इलाज तड़प रहे अपने

पर आशा की किरणें दिखती हैं
आयुष्मान भारत - तस्वीर बदली है
टेलीमेडिसिन, डिजिटल फॉर्म,
स्वास्थ्य सेवा ले रही अब नया नॉर्म।

हर नागरिक को मिले अधिकार,
स्वास्थ्य और शिक्षा हो आधार
ना हो फर्क गाँव-शहर का,
ना हो डर इलाज के खर्च का

भारत बन सकता है मिसाल,
कम लागत में इलाज बेमिसाल।
आओ मिलकर सपना सजाएँ,
'विकसित भारत' की ओर बढ़ जाएँ

Section 5

Law and Order

5.1 Minimum Government, Maximum Governance

The clarion call that continues to resonate in the minds of every concerned Indian is **"Minimum Government, Maximum Governance"**—a promise first made by Prime Minister Narendra Modi in 2014. The US-based economist **Ajay Chhibber** coined the acronym **M2G2** for this philosophy, capturing its essence. The idea emphasizes shrinking the size, structure, and processes of the government while enhancing its efficiency and impact—somewhat reminiscent of the much-hyped **DOGE** initiative launched under the Trump Administration and later handed over to Elon Musk in January 2025.

According to Chhibber, the combined expenditure of India's central and state governments saw a steep rise during the 1980s—by nearly 10 percentage points of GDP, reaching 27% by 1991, and has remained elevated ever since. Today, **government spending hovers around 28% of GDP,** comparable to South Korea but significantly higher than Asian peers like **Thailand, Indonesia, and Vietnam.** Notably, both China and South Korea maintained public spending levels below 20% of GDP during their respective phases of rapid economic expansion, with increases only in recent years.

Reducing the size of government is not only essential to achieving the **fiscal glide path** but also critical for minimizing bureaucratic delays and improving citizen satisfaction. For this to happen, governance structures at both central and state levels must be streamlined and decision-making authority must be decentralized to the **lowest effective administrative tier.** India is poised for accelerated growth—initiating **M2G2** reforms now will ensure the momentum is not lost.

When citizens are forced just to wait and stare,
And hope turns to anger, then to despair,
It's time we act fast,
Make efficiency last
Let "Minimum Government" show that we care!

To cut public costs, can a DOGE-type plan work?
So no Babu has room to delay or shirk?
If work is like prayer,
let service be fair
and progress will flow without a jerk!

सरकार स्वच्छ हो और काम बड़ा करे,
हर गाँव, हर शहर में उजाला भरे

कागज़ों की फाइल अब ना घूमे देर तक,
फैसले हों जल्दी, सरल न्याय की हो दस्तक

बाबू न टाले बात, न मचाए शोर,
जनता को मिले सीधे जवाब हर ओर

छोटे अधिकारी भी लें सही निर्णय,
बिना वजह न रुक जाए संचार का विनिमय

पैसा बचे, काम हो सीधा सादा
नागरिक कहे सरकार निभाती है वादा

कम खर्च, ज़्यादा दम हो शासन में,
देश आगे बढ़े वाकई, न कि बस भाषण में

न हो भीड़ दफ़्तरों के दरवाज़ों पर,
काम हो झटपट अब बस भरोसा कर!

5.2 Parliament in India

IIndia has proudly been a functioning Parliamentary Democracy since Independence. As we move towards 2047, marking 100 years of freedom, it must be our collective resolve to strengthen this vital institution even further.

Our Founding Fathers entrusted Parliament with critical roles: law-making, budget finalization, ensuring financial accountability, and overseeing the executive through debates, questions, and in-depth scrutiny by Parliamentary Committees.

There was a time when the Parliament was a beacon of robust yet respectful discourse — reminiscent of the eloquent exchanges involving legends like Atal Bihari Vajpayee, Piloo Mody, Sitaram Yechury, Sushma Swaraj, and more recently, Shashi Tharoor. Sadly, the spirit of constructive debate has, in recent times, been marred by personal attacks, frequent walkouts, and bills being passed without sufficient high-quality discussion. It is imperative — for elected and nominated members and for us as vigilant citizens — to restore dignity to our parliamentary proceedings.

The road ahead holds transformative changes:

> The **delimitation** process and its potential impact on the composition of Parliament.
>
> **Women's Reservation Bill**, ushering in a significant shift in gender representation.
>
> **'One Nation, One Poll'**, which could reshape the structure and functioning of our elected bodies.
>
> **The rise of a new generation of voters** — sharp, aware, and determined to demand better.

Let us rebuild a future where Parliament is the cornerstone of a vibrant, inclusive, and forward-looking democracy.

The man stood firm on the burning deck,
as debate flared up, a near-fatal wreck.
Can we argue with poise and grace,
not hurl insults all over the place,
In Parliament, after a long, hard trek?

India's a land of vibrant variety,
a fact we celebrate with pride and gaiety.
To our MPs, we earnestly plead,
to rise above, to serve and lead,
and uphold the House with utmost propriety!

भारत की संसद है गर्व का प्रतीक,
जनता की आवाज़ को रखे ये निर्भीक
स्वतंत्रता के बाद से इसकी है पहचान,
2047 तक इसे और मजबूत बनाना – है लक्ष्य महान

विधायिका का कार्य है कानून बनाना,
बजट का अंतिम निर्णय लेना, जिम्मेदारी निभाना
विवादों में भी गरिमा बनाए रखना,
सदनों में शालीनता से बहस करना

विपक्ष की भूमिका है सवाल उठाना,
संसद में अनुशासन को बनाए रखना
विरोध में भी सद्भाव बनाए रखना
सभी सदस्यों का सम्मान करना

भारत के महान नेता, जैसे वाजपेयी, स्वराज, थरूर,
सभी ने संसद को दिया है नई ऊर्जा का जोर।
हर सांसद, हर भारतीय ये संकल्प ले
संसद को गरिमामय बनाये, नई दिशा दें।

आने वाले समय में बदलाव लाने होंगे ,
महिला आरक्षण जैसे अजेंडे अपनाने होंगे
सभी मिलकर देश का भविष्य बनाएं,
संसद की गरिमा को ऊँचा उठाएँ।

5.3 Legal System

The legal system of any country stands as the cornerstone of justice, human rights, and equality before the law. The iconic image of "Insaaf ka Tarazu"—the blindfolded Lady Justice holding a pair of balanced scales—symbolizes what every citizen should expect from the legal process: fairness, impartiality, and swift justice.

Unfortunately, in India, the judicial system is heavily burdened. Courts are grappling with a massive backlog of pending cases, leading to cascading delays and procedural inefficiencies. This long wait often turns the quest for justice into an exhausting ordeal. The situation is further complicated by occasional allegations of corruption—both within the judiciary and law enforcement agencies. In many regions, citizens face significant hurdles even in filing a case, let alone receiving a timely resolution. As the old adage goes, **"Justice delayed is justice denied."**

Structurally, the Indian legal system—rooted in British-era institutions—is well-organized. At the apex is the Supreme Court, followed by High Courts at the state level, and then the subordinate courts (district, civil, and criminal) which handle day-to-day judicial matters. The real challenge lies not in the framework itself, but in the operational flow, accessibility, and implementation.

What we must collectively aspire to is a legal ecosystem where every stakeholder—from lawyers and judges to justices of the High Courts and Supreme Court—is committed to the **speedy and fair** delivery of justice. Only when judgments are passed without undue delay, and the chain from crime to punishment is not stretched endlessly, can we hope for a truly law-abiding, just society.

"Milord," said the lawyer as he rose in court,
"Oh no!" cried the thief, with a startled retort.
He feared a sentence of jail,
but saw delays added to his tale,
Another waiting game, not justice in short.

Justice delayed is justice denied—it's real,
Cases must not drag from reel to reel.
Let the claims be sound,
with evidence profound,
so the law can act and the wounds may heal!

न्याय का मंदिर है यह, सबको अधिकार समान
इंसाफ का तराज़ू थामे, खड़ी है न्यायमूर्ति महान
हर नागरिक को मिले न्याय, यही है इसकी शान
कानून के आगे सब बराबर, यही है इसकी पहचान

सुप्रीम कोर्ट सबसे ऊपर, न्याय का है प्रहरी,
उसके नीचे उच्च न्यायालय, फिर जिला अदालतें कई
कई बार लंबित रहते हैं, मुकदमे सालों सालों तक
न्याय में देरी हो जाए, तो टूटता है सबका सब्र

कभी-कभी भ्रष्टाचार की छाया, पूरे ढांचे को घेरती है
आमजन को न्याय पाने में, मुश्किलें बड़ी आती हैं
पर आशा है हमें अब भी, अवस्था होगी बेहतर,
तेजी से मिलेगा न्याय, हालात अभी हैं बदतर

न्यायपालिका है लोकतंत्र की नींव, ज़रूरी व्यवस्था
हर नागरिक के अधिकारों की करती है रक्षा
न्याय में न हो भेदभाव, यही है सबकी चाह
इंसाफ का सूरज चमके, यही हो भारत की राह

5.4 Law & Order

There's a lot we can both praise and criticize Bollywood for. On the positive side, it has gifted us a sense of patriotism, compelling storytelling, unforgettable romance, and timeless music. On the flip side, however, it has contributed to the spread of negative stereotypes — often misrepresenting certain ethnicities and professions. For instance, veteran actor Mehmood's portrayal of South Indians as "Madrasis," and the long-standing depiction of the average policeman as a pot-bellied, indifferent "Pandu Havildar" have done little to elevate the image of the police force in public perception.

In a country grappling with significant challenges to law and order — including crime, insurgency, terrorism, and organized crime — we must strive to uplift and empower our police system. The force deserves both respect and the kind of necessary authority that mirrors how the NYPD is portrayed in American cinema. Cases of police corruption must be addressed swiftly and transparently. Furthermore, adequate infrastructure, resources, and a responsive legal system are essential if the public is to truly respect, and fear, the consequences of breaking the law.

As a nation, we must commit to doing more. We cannot allow fear to grip our cities — tourists avoiding certain regions, or women hesitating to step out alone at night, even in the national capital, Delhi. Police reforms, judicial accountability, and community policing are key steps in building a safer, more just society. These measures will foster trust and collaboration between citizens and the forces meant to protect them.

The phrase *"Kanoon ke haath lambe hote hain"* is a popular Bollywood cliché — but it's time we turned that into a lived reality, where the laws reach is truly firm, fair, and respected by all.

Danda in hand, white shirt and khaki pants,
the havaldar and inspector trade long-winded rants.
While victims wait and justice stalls,
in crumbling rooms with faded walls,
still hoping someone hears their chants.

In this land of justice and liberty,
we must rise as one — every she and he.
Let's honour the law and support the cop,
Strengthen the system till the last drop,
to build a just and viksit country.

बॉलीवुड ने पुलिस को, कभी नायक तो कभी खलनायक बनाया,
कभी हँसते-मुस्कराते पांडु हवलदार का चेहरा दिखाया।
कहीं ईमानदार अफसर, तो कहीं भ्रष्टाचार की छाया,
कभी डर, कभी भरोसा, पुलिस का रूप बदलता आया।

कानून के हाथ लंबे हैं, सुनते हैं फिल्मों में बार-बार,
पर असल ज़िंदगी में न्याय की राह है बहुत ही दुश्वार
कभी पुलिस पर आरोप लगे, कभी जनता ने नकार दिया
भ्रष्टाचार और हिंसा ने, छवि को और धुंधला किया

फिर भी कई अफसर हैं, जो करते हैं ईमानदारी से काम,
जनता की सुरक्षा में प्रस्तुत, सेवा करते हैं निष्काम
समाज और पुलिस का रिश्ता, विश्वास से बनता है मजबूत,
समुदाय की भागीदारी से, कानून का राज होता है पूर्ण

महिलाओं की सुरक्षा, बच्चों की मुस्कान ज़रूरी है,
डर के साये में रहना क्यों इनकी मजबूरी है?
आओ मिलकर करें प्रयास, सुधारें पुलिस की व्यवस्था,
न्याय, सुरक्षा, और विश्वास से, बने विकास का रास्ता

5.5 Cyber Crimes

This is a story most of us in India have encountered at least once in the past year. One of us received a call from someone claiming to be from the Crime Branch. The caller said a shipment containing contraband substances had been found—addressed in our name. An arrest team, they warned, was on its way—unless we took "urgent action."

Despite the wave of fear that naturally followed, we had the presence of mind to ask for proof. The caller quickly sent a photo of a police officer. Still skeptical, we decided to visit the cyber-crime unit ourselves—only to be laughed at and told to ignore such scams!

These "Jamtara-style" incidents, where the caller instructs you to press a certain number (usually 9) for further steps, are blatant attempts to extort money from innocent citizens. The frightening reality, however, is that these hoaxes are evolving—now involving deepfake audio and video to make them even more convincing.

Cyber-crimes today target both individuals and businesses. From phishing emails and data theft to malware attacks that can bring entire systems to a standstill, the threats are real and growing. Temporary disruptions in networks, hijacked communications, and stolen identities have become alarmingly common.

As we stride toward becoming a *Viksit Bharat* (developed nation), we must build stronger cyber-security frameworks. It is crucial to implement robust data protection laws and privacy practices. The integrity of our digital systems—especially those running major organizations—cannot be compromised. While the integration of technology in our personal and professional lives is a positive trend, it also demands that we stay alert, informed, and protected. Let's keep the cyber-crooks out and ensure that our lives and businesses continue without disruption.

If you want to stay out of jail, press nine,
the caller's voice was urgent, cold, and fine.
I nearly fell for the cunning trap—
a cybercrime dressed in legal wrap—
till the cops said, "Relax. You're doing just fine!"

Crooks now lurk on the internet with flair,
Sending malware, scams, and digital scare.
Let's shield our data, stay alert and wise,
with firewalls strong and watchful eyes,
to keep our systems safe with utmost care!

रामू बैठा था घर में, मोबाइल बजा अचानक,
अनजान नंबर से आई कॉल, आवाज़ थी बड़ी सख्त
"मैं हूँ क्राइम ब्रांच से, तेरे नाम पर केस बना है,
अगर बात न मानी, तो पुलिस ने लेके जाना है!"

रामू का दिल धड़का, माथे पर आया पसीना,
तुरंत भेज दी फोटो, एक अफसर की वर्दी में सीना
कहा "अगर बचना है, तो अभी नंबर नौ दबाओ,"
रामू ने समझदारी से साइबर पुलिस को बुलाया

साइबर पुलिस हँसी, बोली "डरना नहीं,
ये नए ज़माने के ठग हैं, इनसे बचना है सही"
"कभी OTP, कभी बैंक डिटेल, किसी से भी मत कहना,
फर्जी लिंक, अजनबी कॉल, इनसे बचना ही है कहना"

तकनीक है वरदान, पर खतरे भी हैं साथ,
जागरूक रहो, सतर्क रहो, न सुनो इनकी बात
साइबर पुलिस मदद को तैयार है हर बार
सजग नागरिक बनो, सुरक्षा हो अपने अधिकार

Section 6

Entrepreneurship

6.1 Entrepreneurship–Developing the Mindset

The clarion call of **"Startup India, Stand up India"** inspired a wave of young aspirants to dive into the world of entrepreneurship. Some entered with genuine capability and determination, others with a great idea and a dash of optimism, while many plunged in without a clear understanding of the market, a viable business model, sufficient capital, a solid team, or most importantly, the true entrepreneurial mindset.

As expected, many early ventures faltered, their dreams left by the wayside. Yet, a few emerged victorious—becoming the legends and role models for the next generation of entrepreneurs. At the heart of success, lies **a mindset rooted in clarity and purpose**—a deep understanding of a distinct market opportunity, coupled with a differentiated product or service idea with the potential to be a market leader—or even a category creator.

Today, many AI startups are pushing boundaries with solutions unimaginable a decade ago. But success demands more than just innovation. It requires a well-defined customer segment, establishing product-market fit and visibility into at least the next two rounds of funding. These enable a startup to build a strong team, scale operations, and pursue sustainable growth.

As India continues its journey of rapid economic growth, immense opportunities will arise—not just in emerging sectors like **AI, Electric Mobility, Shared Transportation**, and **Automation**, but also in gaps created by shifting capabilities. Success will come to those who can **strategically map their pathways,** navigate challenges, and ride the waves of transformation.

Young folks often want to chart their own course,
not sit in jobs that lack fire or force.
But startups aren't for the faint of heart—
you need grit, not just a flashy start,
and must work 70 hours, with no remorse!

Starting up may sound bold and cool,
till the world thinks you've lost in a duel
But when the venture begins to thrive,
and both funders and customers high-five—
Even critics cheer and say, "Yes! That's the jewel!"

तो आगे क्या विचार है?
परीक्षा में तो कुछ ख़ास किया नहीं
लक्षण ठीक नहीं, असफलता के आसार हैं

सरकरी नौकरी, नौकरी कोई भी मिल जाए
नौकरी न मिली तो क्या होगा
अब ना ये चिंता रहे, हुनर पर भरोसा आये

नौकर नहीं किसी के, मालिक हों हम
तकनीक, हिम्मत और जागृति दिखाएं
शान से खुद के उद्योग धंधे के कर्ता हों हम

माहौल देश में बन चुका, अब और परवान चढ़े
सहायता और सहयोग के नए सोपान हों
निर्भर किसी पर नहीं, स्वयं के स्वामी बन बढ़ें

6.2 Entrepreneurship–Building Ecosystems

There is perhaps no better example of successful ecosystem building than India's $220 billion IT services industry. When one of the authors, Ganesh, joined the sector and became an entrepreneur-CEO at **APTECH** in 1991, the industry was worth only a few hundred crores, with just a handful of companies.

A pivotal partnership between the then-nascent industry association **NASSCOM** (National Association of Software and Services Companies) and the Department of Electronics (which later became the Ministry of Electronics and Information Technology – **MeitY**) laid the foundation for exponential growth. Their joint initiative led to the creation of **Software Technology Parks of India (STPI)** in key cities, giving rise to a new generation of tech entrepreneurs.

As small companies began to scale, the **venture capital** and later **private equity** industries flourished, fueling innovation and growth. The ecosystem has expanded to include multiple verticals: **IT services, software products and platforms, Business Process Management (BPM), Engineering Services, and Global Capability Centres (GCCs)** — each employing millions and contributing to India's incredible digital success story.

Ecosystem creation, however, is never accidental. It is the result of **carefully planned and collaborative efforts**, involving the **central and state governments, large enterprises, capital providers, research and academic institutions,** and, most importantly, the **entrepreneurs themselves.** Today, similar ecosystems are emerging in **automobile manufacturing, electronics clusters,** and new-age sectors like **microprocessors and electric mobility.** For India's entrepreneurial momentum to shape the future, these ecosystems must be actively **nurtured and scaled.**

When a bunch of mavericks
Come up with new tricks,
do they stop and ponder
if the success yonder
will come from bits and bytes—or bricks?

Entrepreneurs always have the will to create,
but need more to get out of the starting gate.
Ecosystems must emerge,
as all interests converge,
to shape bold ventures and make them great!

ये कहानी तो सभी ने सुनी है
कैसे अकेली लकड़ी तुरंत टूट जाए
और साथ हों कई सारी तो
कितनी ही ताकत लगा लो, न टूट पाएं

उद्यमिता एक जूनून है
लेकिन बड़ी है ज़िम्मेदारी
अकेला नहीं चला पायेगा
बोझ से भरी है गाड़ी

जो साथ मिले उद्यमी को अच्छा
फिर देखो उसकी हिम्मत
पंख सपने फैलाएंगे
सतत निरंतर करता मेहनत

देश नयी ऊंचाइयों पर
सबका साथ सबका विकास
सहूलियत दे दो उद्योगी को बस
वो कर लेगा बाकी प्रयास!

6.3 Entrepreneurship – Succeeding Through Orbits

How often do we see a start-up rise with early success, bask in a blaze of glory, and then—just as quickly—fade away? After reaching an initial peak, many find themselves unable to scale further, acquire new customers, or break past the first plateau.

And yet, there are exceptions. Take the example of Zensar—a company one of us has been closely associated with for over a decade. Zensar managed to scale through multiple orbits of growth: from ₹0 to ₹10 crores, then ₹10 to ₹100 crores, ₹100 to ₹1,000 crores, and beyond. The first orbit was driven by a deep focus on Oracle technologies and applications, while the second orbit saw geographic expansion and service diversification, using a "Follow the Customer" strategy

The key differentiator? The wisdom behind the phrase: **"What got you here won't get you there."** The ability to pivot, evolve, and rethink business models is what separates hyper-scalers from the also-rans. As India sets its sights on achieving over 8% annual GDP growth until 2047, thousands of start-ups must not only succeed in terms of revenues, profits, and market share—but must also develop the courage to challenge their past formulas and launch new value propositions. They must continuously leap into new growth curves, into new **sigmoid waves** of innovation and reinvention.

The question is: Are today's entrepreneurs ready for this relentless evolution?

Well begin is half done
But when you are in for the long run
A great entrepreneurial start
is not really the best part
For a team that aims for the sun.

One the first customer lets you begin
And with every new client there is a din
Remember that a great start
Is just the first chapter in the fine art
To new deals and growth with every win.

एक स्टार्टअप ने सपनों के साथ उड़ान भरी,
शुरुआती सफलता से हर आँख में चमक जगी
पर पहली मंज़िल के बाद ही थम गया कारवां,
नए ग्राहक न मिले, रुक गया सफर वहाँ

कुछ ने सीखा, बदली राह, नया orbit चुना,
बिजनेस मॉडल बदला, नवाचार को गले लगाया
जैसे ज़ेन्सार ने हर बार नई ऊँचाई पाई,
फोकस, विविधता ने सफलता की सीढ़ी चढ़ाई

सिर्फ़ पहली जीत पर रुकना नहीं, यही है असली बात
हर पड़ाव के बाद चाहिए नया प्रयास, नया साथ
जो बदलते हैं समय संग, वही असली विजेता बनते,
हर orbit में नयी ऊर्जा से, आगे बढ़ते रहते

6.4 Entrepreneurship – Opportunity Share

IIt was the legendary Professor C.K. Prahalad, in his landmark book Competing for the Future, who first introduced the concept of **"Opportunity Share."** He argued that competing for a larger share in an existing, crowded marketplace can be an uphill battle—every percentage point is hard-won. In contrast, entrepreneurs who innovate to **create a new market** or **disrupt an existing one** can achieve **exponential growth** and unlock immense value.

History is full of examples of visionaries who chose the **path less traveled** and went on to build extraordinary success stories. Globally, we celebrate names like **Steve Jobs** (Apple), **Jeff Bezos** (Amazon), and **Elon Musk** (Tesla & SpaceX). Closer to home, we have inspiring stories like **Vijay Shekhar Sharma** (PayTM) and **Sridhar Vembu** (Zoho), who disrupted conventional spaces and pioneered their own.

There are also examples of **seizing segment-specific** opportunities through innovative service models. Companies like **APTECH,** with its global franchising model, and **Zensar**, with its Solution Blueprinting and Blueprint Foundries, rewrote the rules of growth and carved out significant opportunity share.

As the global market opens up for Indian entrepreneurs across sectors, the key lies in being **inventive with product and service ideas and innovative in go-to-market strategies.** The government is actively looking to back **Champion companies**—both established leaders and emerging innovators capable of writing new success stories.

The stage is set. The time is now. For India's youth, it's the **land of limitless opportunity**—ripe for those ready to rise and shine!

The pundits say – go for market share
But when preferences shift, customers don't care
When the product wont move at any price
Its important to move beyond the initial surprise
And new horzons the entrepreneur must dare.

When old ideas are seen as done
There are many new battles yet to be won
lets find what new customers will desire
It doesn't take long for the engines to fire
And the bold entrpreneur to find a place in the sun.

जो चलें भीड़ से अलग, वही अवसर पाते हैं,
नव विचार, नव बाज़ार, दुनिया में छा जाते हैं

सी.के. प्रह्लाद ने कहा, अवसर की पहचान करो,
जहाँ बाज़ार नया मिले, वहीं अपनी उड़ान भरो

स्टीव जॉब्स, एलन मस्क, या फिर बेज़ोस का नाम,
नवाचार की राह चुन, रचा इन्होंने इतिहास महान

विजय शेखर, श्रीधर वेंबू ने भी यही दिखाया,
अद्भुत सोच से भारत का परचम लहराया

नयी सेवा, नया मॉडल, नयी सोच का मेल,
बदलते बाज़ार में यही है सफलता का खेल

संघर्ष से न घबराओ, अवसर की तलाश करो,
अपने विश्वास से, हर असंभव को संभव करो

सरकार भी चाहती है, नए चैंपियन का निर्माण,
युवाओं के स्टार्टअप जोश से बढ़ेगा देश का मान

बाज़ार की भीड़ में मत उलझो, कुछ अलग सोचो,
रोज़गार निर्माण करो, नवाचार की राह खोजो

6.5 Entrepreneurship – Students' Bridge to Bharat

The phrase **"Catch them young"** holds true in many areas — especially when it comes to identifying and nurturing entrepreneurs. There was a time when the first priority for graduates from premier institutes like the Indian Institutes of Technology (IITs) and Indian Institutes of Management (IIMs) was to secure a job with giants like Unilever, Tata Administrative Services, or McKinsey. Then the trend shifted towards investment banking and private equity firms. Today, many of our brightest students are eager to dive into startups, sometimes even before graduating.

However, encouraging entrepreneurship among underprepared students presents a dual challenge. First, academic institutions may use entrepreneurship as an excuse to ease off their responsibility of helping students find good jobs. Second, enthusiastic but inexperienced youth — with stars in their eyes but without a clear product or business plan or access to capital — often leap prematurely and fail within months.

Thankfully, organizations like the GTT Foundation with its **"Bridge to Bharat"** Student Entrepreneurship initiative, along with incubators and accelerators like **ARISE, IIT Bombay's SINE, T-HUB, and TiE's Nurture program** — are addressing this gap. They are systematically identifying promising entrepreneurs, training them to refine their ideas, clarify objectives, and develop strategies. They assist students in finalizing products or services and charting a path from product development to market success.

As the saying goes, many a "slip between the cup and the lip" — student entrepreneurship is a noble goal, but it must be nurtured carefully to guide young talent toward real success.

"Start up India, Stand up India" rings clear in my ear,
I quit my desk job with excitement — no fear!
No time to prepare,
Just leap in the air,
But quick failure came, greeted by jeers.

Next time, young dreamers, take note:
Entrepreneurship needs more than just hope.
Great ideas, capital, a strong team,
A market to serve — not just a dream.
Let's find and support young talent to help them cope!

छात्र जीवन में ही जाग जाएँ जो अच्छे विचार
तो उद्यमिता है, सपनों को पंख देने को तैयार
नौकरी की राह अब पुरानी सी लगे,
स्टार्टअप की दुनिया की ललक सी जगे

आईआईटी, आईआईएम से युवा
अब खुद की पहचान बनाने प्रेरित हुआ
नवाचार की लौ लेकर बढ़ते हैं आगे,
रोज़गार नहीं, अब रोजगार देने की चाहत जागे

हर चुनौती को स्वीकार कर रहे हैं,
संस्थाएँ भी साथ खड़ी हो रही हैं
मार्गदर्शन, निवेश, प्रशिक्षण का संग,
हर छात्र को मिल रही है नया उमंग

गाँव से शहर तक, सेतु बन रहे हैं,
GTT, SINE, T-Hub, TiE--- बहुत मेहनत कर रहे हैं
कभी असफलता, कभी सफलता की बयार,
हर अनुभव से मिलता है नया आधार।

युवाओं की ऊर्जा से बदल रहा है भारत,
हर कोना, हर गाँव बन रहा है समर्थ।
छात्र उद्यमिता से खिल रही है नई आशा,
युवाओं के जोश से सजेगा भारत का भविष्य सच्चा।

SECTION 7

People

7.1 Education

Since Independence, successive Governments in India have focused on improving the quality of education, especially for underserved communities. Our work at the Foundation to Educate Girls has highlighted the very poor quality of educational resources available in rural and tribal areas across many States. In states like Rajasthan, Madhya Pradesh, Uttar Pradesh, and Bihar, the dropout rates among girls remain alarmingly high, with families often lacking motivation to send girls to school beyond primary education.

In recent years, initiatives such as **"Beti Padhao Beti Bachao"** and **"Sarva Shiksha Abhiyan"** have made significant strides in addressing these challenges. State Governments have increased education budgets and expanded the Open School system to help children continue their studies. However, much still needs to be done to ensure consistent quality and seamless progression from primary to secondary and tertiary education.

A nation can truly call itself developed only when access to quality education becomes a guaranteed right for every citizen. It is crucial to enhance both the quantity and quality of teacher training institutes, adopt innovative teaching tools and technologies, implement modern pedagogies, and strengthen governance at all levels of the education system. This will help realize a **"no child left behind"** approach across every State.

In higher education, recent efforts have introduced liberal arts education as a promising alternative to traditional Arts, Science, and Commerce streams. Institutions like **FLAME** and **ASHOKA** are establishing themselves as viable models of this new approach. For India to succeed on the global stage, a robust and inclusive education model must emerge—one that nurtures creativity, critical thinking, and lifelong learning for all.

In India, it's complicated to be a child,
Uncertain if the world's gentle or wild.
Whether suffering in a village class,
or polishing household brass,
The paths to success seem narrow, not wide.

As a nation, we must all educate
every child who wants to enter the school gate.
No excuses for those who keep kids near,
let's help our children, with vision clear,
and support their quest to be great!

आंख खुली और खुद को पाया एक मायाजाल में
सब खुश थे लेकिन आशंकित उस दिन अस्पताल में

क्या बनेगा बड़ा होकर, क्या करेगा ये पढ़ाई
क्या शिक्षा लेगा ये या चलाएगा करछी कढ़ाई ?

सवाल सही है, हर बच्चे का अधिकार है शिक्षा
सरकारों ने खोले हैं द्वार, दी जाए सभी को विद्या

शिक्षा के आयाम कई, नहीं सिर्फ ज़रिया कमाई का
विकास में बड़ा हिस्सा है, देश के बच्चों की पढ़ाई का

बच्चियां हो, बालक हों, या हों प्रतिभाशाली युवा
बिन शिक्षा के नहीं किसी भी राष्ट्र का सपना पूरा हुआ

शिक्षा पर ध्यान हो पूरा, नहीं इस से कोई अधिक बलवान
साक्षर नहीं सुशिक्षित बने, हर बच्चा है राष्ट्र की पहचान

7.2 Agency for Children and Youth

In a country where hundreds of millions still grow up in poor villages and crowded city slums, simply surviving childhood and youth traumas to become responsible members of society is a huge challenge. Even if we live in a city like Pune for decades, we may never truly understand the struggles faced by young people in the six hundred slum communities scattered across the city. But the more important question is: **do these children and youth have any agency — the power to take ownership of their own lives?**

Organizations like Akanksha and Teach for India have launched impactful interventions across the country, bringing joy and hope to schoolchildren through both in-class and after-school programs. Meanwhile, Lighthouse Communities Foundation offers a free six-week agency development program in five Indian states that helps youth overcome their fears and empowers them to dream — just like every child deserves.

For India to truly succeed, we must open minds to dream and aspire, show clear pathways to choose their own goals, and help realize those dreams through meaningful employment or entrepreneurship. This is the gift every child and youth deserves. When young people gain this ability to envision and achieve their dreams, it transforms not just their lives, but the happiness of their families and entire communities — reducing conflict and building harmony.

Great nations are built by committed citizens. This is the mission we must embrace to make a **Viksit Bharat** a reality!

"What's the point?" the young man cried,
if my plans have withered and died?
Did you ever care to see
what dreams live inside me?
You never asked — you never tried!"

"Give me the chance to dream my dream,
then ask me about my chosen stream.
If I live in fear,
Doing work I don't hold dear,
I'll just pass time — never be part of your team!"

बहुत हिम्मत है, आसमान में सूराख बनाने हैं मुझे
अपने घर परिवार के लिए, चिराग जलाने हैं मुझे

अकसर बच्चा या युवा सोच रखता है कुछ ऐसी
पर सिस्टम के चक्कर में, दिशा नहीं मिलती वैसी

हर कोई बस लीक पर चलने पर मजबूर है
कान आंख पर बांधे पट्टी, मानो वो मजदूर है

ऐसे कैसे बढ़त मिलेगी, दुनिया में संसार में
कैसे झेलेगा चुनौतियां काम पे और व्यापार में

भूख युवा की नहीं दबानी, बल्कि और बढ़ानी है
जूनून तो उस में है ही, उसे बस अच्छी राह दिखानी है

उत्साह, रचनात्मकता को खुल कर व्यक्त कर पाए
देश बढ़ेगा तभी जब युवा पीढ़ी आत्मविश्वास दिखाए

उछालने दो उसे पत्थर, क्लर्की में मत फंसाओ
उसे बनाओ विचारक, उसे नौकर बनना मत सिखाओ

7.3 Skills

India has been working on skilling its youth for many decades, yet the challenge remains unresolved. Even today, many young people who complete skills programs find themselves unemployed or underemployed. Meanwhile, thousands of job opportunities remain unfilled because candidates with the right skills are simply not available.

Traditional blue-collar skills in manufacturing—such as plumbing and fitting—have evolved; giving way to advanced areas like CNC machining, robotics, and the manufacturing and maintenance of electric vehicles (EVs). Aspirations have also shifted from basic computer programming and testing toward analytics, artificial intelligence, and data sciences. Additionally, emerging fields such as environmental sustainability are creating new job families.

Both existing and future sectors will require a combination of formal education and on-the-job training. The National Skills Development Corporation (NSDC) has played a crucial role by establishing sector skills councils focused on training and certification. The remarkable success of the Future Skills Program, launched by the government and industry association NASSCOM, demonstrates that when youth agency is aligned with actual job opportunities, livelihoods abound.

Lighthouse Communities Foundation has pioneered a comprehensive seven-part model encompassing mobilization, agency development, counseling, core skills building, soft skills training, placement, and on-the-job retention. Numerous initiatives like this aim to cultivate aspiration and livelihood skills among underprivileged youth in both urban and rural areas. These efforts will need to coexist alongside advanced courses accessible to the urban well-to-do, ensuring that India becomes a nation of skilled, aspirational individuals ready for employment and entrepreneurship in the years ahead.

They took us up the mountain called "New Skills,"
Hoping we'd catch the names and feel the thrills.
But are there jobs for us?
Or will we miss the bus
to a livelihood that truly pays the bills?

We know too well the crowd that chases jobs,
Seeking meaning, not wrenching out sobs.
"Make me ready," we say—
to ride the gravy train one day,
in a field I choose, not Raja's or Bob's!

क्या मॉडल है सफलता का ?
काम और धन मिले और मिले सम्मान ?
पर जो संतुष्टि हुनर से मिले
बताओ उसका कहाँ है नाम ?

सिर्फ पास कर दसवीं बारहवीं
कहाँ कोई कुछ बन पाता है
सीख के नयी कोई कला ही
हर कोई आगे बढ़ पाता है

अगर देश को चलना है
प्रगति पथ पर बहुत ही तेज़
तो मिलकर आगे करना होगा
हुनर विकास से न कोई गुरेज़

नयी नयी स्किल्स सुझाकर
आज के युवा का सिंचन करें
नित नयी तकनीकें देकर
जोश की नयी हुंकार भरें

बहुत हुआ है, अभी बहुत है
काम इस दिशा में होना
युवा अगर बन गया सुदृढ़
भारत भूमि फिर उगलेगी सोना !

7.4 Internships

The opportunity to take up and learn from a good internship has long been a valuable part of superior academic institutions like BITS Pilani and NITIE (now IIM) Mumbai. Internships should be seen as a preparatory program for full-time jobs—not a weak substitute. In recent years, internships in India have become more formalized through initiatives like the Prime Minister's Internship Scheme, the NITI Aayog Internship Scheme, the Digital India Internship Scheme, and many others, with corporates encouraged to offer them widely.

So, what sets a good internship apart from a summer project or even an entry-level job in a large organization? For starters, an internship is defined by both clear activities and tangible outcomes to be completed within a fixed period—not just observing and learning passively on the job. It builds confidence in young people and encourages them to experiment and find their own solutions.

The future of India rests on leveraging our demographic dividend and empowering youth to discover their confidence early, so they can leave their mark in whatever vocation they choose. Indians can learn from examples in the West, where college isn't just an assembly line but one option among many. Many young people choose internships after high school, gain valuable experience and income for a few years, and then decide their next steps. With agency, skills, and a meaningful internship, the sky is the limit for our youth.

Get up and go the factory next door,
Do a project—don't just watch the shop floor.
Its part of your course, you know—
whether you learn or have something to show.
For students and colleges, it's this and no more.

Compare that with the joys of an intern:
To jump right in, not await your turn.
A chance for real learning,
with outcomes and meaning—
Internships warm you, they don't make you burn!

करोगे तो सीखोगे, ये मूलमंत्र है भाई
शुक्र है सीखने की उम्र नहीं बताई

निकल पड़ो घर से बाहर, देखो कैसे होता है काम
केवल किताबों में नहीं कैद, दुनिया में है ज्ञान तमाम

आज के युवा तभी बढ़ेंगे, जब जूते चटखायेंगे
आरामों में रह गए तो, क्या फिर ये सीख पाएंगे?

शिक्षा नहीं मोहताज किताब की, न ही पेशा शिक्षा पर निर्भर
देश और खुद के विकास को, चले युवा गर निडर

तभी होगा कल्याण सभी का, तभी तो ज्ञान का मतलब है
इतनी ऊर्जा जो है युवा में, कुछ नया करने की तलब है

प्रोजेक्ट और इंटर्नशिप को गंभीरता से लेना होगा
फ़ायदा इसका समझना होगा, दिल से अपनाना होगा!

7.5 Social Mobility

There was a time soon after independence when a successful life meant studying as much and as long as the family could afford, taking the first available job, and ideally staying in it until retirement. The picture was not too different in the West either, where the classic American way of life was a factory worker returning home to an adoring wife holding an infant and a toddler clinging to her hand, with the family dog running around the yard.

In India, the deeply stratified social system meant that very few people aspired to move out of their social strata. There was no expectation that the maid or the driver in the household would ever dream of moving up in society. Fortunately, this mindset has changed dramatically. Today, every Indian aspires for their children to surpass their social circle and use education as a beanstalk to climb the social ladder.

Jerry, a driver in Mumbai whom we know, resolved to finish his graduation and later joined the administrative ranks of his organization. In a country bursting with soaring aspirations, Jerry will no longer be an exception. The horizon of opportunity is now open to all who dare to dream and work hard for the tools needed to make their social mobility dreams come true. Already, IIT campuses are full of middle-class youth determined to compete and succeed against the best in the world, while some privileged youth choose to fly abroad for education rather than cracking competitive exams. Both paths have their merits, but the critical point is that there should be no ceiling for any aspiring citizen of our country!

IIs this just another tale of Tom and Jerry,
Where Tom the postman delivers letters and makes merry,
While Jerry the driver decides to study,
Suddenly, he becomes your office buddy!
Social mobility – that's the sweet cherry!

In a country where everyone's hopes are bright,
There's no room for those who drop out of sight,
We owe it to ourselves to rise and shine,
Work our way up, not whine or recline,
And grab every chance to scale new career heights!

राजा का बेटा राजा
और सुनार का हो सुनार
गए ज़माने इन बातों के
अब बदलाव की है बयार

उन्नत समाज का ये है ढंग
जो चाहे वो बढ़ सकता है
जिसमें हो जज़्बा जैसा भी
कोई भी काम वो कर सकता है

पढ़ लिख कर नहीं केवल
हुनर किसी का जाना जाए
गर जूनून हो, और होशियारी
आगे आगे वो बढ़ता जाए

कोई रोक नहीं लगन को
इच्छा करे तो बढ़ेगा आगे
देश हमारा कर रहा प्रगति
युवा करते हैं मेहनत के वादे !

Section 8

Love & Inclusion

8.1 Pride in Being LGBTQ!

When we visited Bermuda at the end of summer 2024, one of the first sights we witnessed was a vibrant and joyous PRIDE parade winding through the streets of Hamilton, the island's capital. Marchers, decorated trucks, genuinely happy couples, and enthusiastic onlookers all came together to celebrate a community that, while so much like everyone else, courageously dared to be different.

Growing up in a state where homosexuality was often silenced, and with several friends in college who were gay, I used to think of it as something to be ashamed of. The comparison was always made between "normal" people and couples versus those who were different. Thankfully, we have come a long way since then.

In India, it is estimated that about ten percent of the population identifies as Lesbian, Gay, Bisexual, Transgender, or Queer (LGBTQ), although only around twenty percent of them are open about their identity and preferences. This percentage may be higher in urban areas, where there is increasing acceptance of live-in relationships and same-sex partnerships. Transgender identities have been a part of Indian culture for centuries, and while some people may still feel uncomfortable, by and large, LGBTQ individuals are gaining acceptance in workplaces, even if social acceptance remains a work in progress.

For a truly *Viksit Bharat* (developed India), it is crucial to ensure that every person is accepted for who they are—not for who they want to be or whom they choose to marry. Europe and the USA can serve as inspiring models in making LGBTQ acceptance a genuine, nationwide phenomenon.

Walking through New York's Columbia University,
I passed by washrooms labeled "Not Sure," "She," and "He."
Gay marriages in the park,
and relationships open, not just in the dark—
all types living together in perfect harmony.

LGBTQ, goes the oft-repeated patter,
Sexuality is not a weapon to batter.
The "He" or the "Male"
Who wants to be "Female"—
In a developed nation, does it really matter?

कोई सीरियस बीमारी है क्या?
या बस दिमाग का फितूर है
ये ज़माने के बाइनरी से अलग
कैसा अजीब दस्तूर है?

अरे छोड़ दी हैं ये दकियानूसी बातें!
हमने ज़माने की नब्ज़ को पहचाना है
निजी पसंद – नापसन्दों को हमने
खुले दिल से स्वीकारा है

दफ्तर हों या सामाजिक जीवन
हर जगह सबकी सुनवाई है
आदमी औरत के परे भी
प्रेम प्यार लगाव की ख़ुदाई है

कोई किसी को भी चाहे
भारत में वो कोई पाप नहीं
प्रगति मेहनत से होती है
लैंगिकता का कोई हाथ नहीं

कोई नर हो, नारी या फिर अन्य कोई
लक्ष्य ये है कि आगे बढ़ते चलें
नए भारत का हर कोई निर्माता है
क्यों फिर ये लड़ाई फ़िज़ूल की लड़ें ?

8.2 A Land without Fear for Women

Anyone who has grown up in India will recall, with a mix of dread and sorrow, at least two horrific cases of rape and murder that dominated media headlines for days—sometimes even weeks. One haunting incident that still lingers is the kidnapping and brutal murder of two innocent children in Delhi in 1978, Sanjay and Geeta Chopra, and the subsequent arrest and imprisonment of the perpetrators, "Billa and Ranga."

Thanks to the widespread reach of television and social media, the infamous "Nirbhaya" case—a brutal gang rape and murder of a young woman on a moving bus in Delhi—sparked a wave of national outrage and protests. It also ignited a collective resolve, at least in many Indian cities, which such inhumane acts against women must stop.

Then, almost unexpectedly, came the "Abhaya" case in Kolkata—a city that has always prided itself on protecting and venerating women, a place where the Goddess Kali is worshipped above all else. This brutal incident shook the entire nation to its core once again.

India needs a catharsis—at least fifteen to twenty years of deep attitudinal change in both men and women, combined with strict punishments for verbal and physical violence against women—to create a truly safe environment. We must urgently re-examine our beliefs and attitudes toward women for any meaningful change to take root.

Stop objectifying women, stop passing judgment on their clothing, behavior, or attitude. Only when every Indian truly believes in equality will a society of respect and safety for women emerge.

Let us reflect, we men,
if indeed, as and when,
we pass comment,
without lament,
Is it bias towards women?

We as a nation must progress,
and for that, we cannot regress.
In love and inclusion
lies our true mission—
for equality, strive more, not less!

अब घर से निकलने से पहले वो आइना तो देखती है
लेकिन पहले सी दहशत अब उसके प्राण नहीं सोखती है
क्या पहना है, कितने बजे हैं, क्यों निकली वो इतनी रात
मुस्कुरा रही है वो क्योंकि अब कोई नहीं पूछता ऐसी बात

खुल के सांस लेने पर अब लफंगे सीटियां नहीं बजाते हैं
खाली सड़क, बस, सूना हॉल देख माँ बाप अब नहीं घबराते है
अब देवी पूजने वाले कन्या को भी पूज रहे
सम्मान और समानता की ये कठिन पहेली बूझ रहे

उन्नत समाज, सच्चा विकास, समझ का संचार जन जन में हो रहा
वाकई विश्वगुरु बना है देश न्यायिक बराबरी, लैंगिक समानता दे रहा
अब अपने हिस्से के आसमान में वो खूब उड़ानें भरती है
अब नहीं कहता उस से कोई "बेटी, बलात्कार तो तेरी ही गलती है"

8.3 Atrocities on Minorities

What makes us believe that minorities in our country are "children of a lesser God"? When a comedian at a 2024 US Presidential election rally cracked a joke laced with racial prejudice, he—and indeed the entire campaign—was roasted on social media. Yet, Vice President Nimee Vance responded by saying, "America should stop taking everything so seriously!"

In our country, however, the time has truly come to take every barb, every insult, and every blow inflicted on any member or group of a minority community very seriously. For a nation aspiring to be a major thought leader from the Global South and a role model for the world, it is unimaginable that twenty percent of its citizens remain marginalized simply due to an accident of birth or a choice of religion.

Too often, we witness acts of violence that breed anger and retaliation, deepening the fissures created by age-old prejudices and false stereotypes about people and places. These acts do nothing but widen the divide and stunt our collective progress.

So, how do we—thoughtful, well-meaning Indians—encourage a whole generation of skeptics and divisive voices to shift their attitudes toward a climate of love and inclusion? If not in themselves, then at least for the sake of the next generation.

We must reject all forms of "othering" and extend many friendly overtures to build a climate of trust, brotherhood, and shared humanity in our communities and across our country. Let us envision a land where caste, class, or community hold no sway over how we treat one another—as human beings.

Towards this ideal, let us resolve to progress together.

The lad stood firm on a burning stage,
his pain too deep to gauge,
Unable to defend,
against those who offend,
Who roam the streets to wreck and pillage.

Can we start anew with love and inclusion,
and not wait for divine intervention?
Call out the wicked who play the game,
and show regret for past shame—
now let us bring forth the peaceful dove's mission.

वो कोने में बैठी देख रही थी अचरज से
हर कोई उस से बात कर रहा था अदब से

न कोई परेशानी थी उसे इस दफ्तर में
काम उसका सब हो रहा था रफ़्तार में

न उसकी जाती को लेकर कोई सवाल
न धर्म पर किसी ने किया कोई बवाल

उसको कायदे से सारे नियम बताये गए
एक भी बार नहीं कोई ताने सुनाये गए

वो हैरान थी, उसे तो आदत थी दुर्व्यवहार की
जात पात और मज़हब से बदलते व्यवहार की

बाप दादाओं ने ऊँची जाती वालों से मार तक खायी
घर परिवार की महिलाओं ने झेली थी पिटाई

लेकिन विकास ने ऐसी कमाल की लहर चलायी
जाति और धर्म कोई भी हो, नहीं है कोई रुसवाई

अब भारत मेरा वाकई में सबकी खातिर महान है
बराबरी से ये वतन मेरा भी, और मेरा भी जहान है!

8.4 Towards Gender Equality!

What makes many men in India believe that different rules apply to men and women? In small towns and rural areas, we often hear of harsh punishments meted out to women by their own families and village leaders simply for falling in love with someone outside their community. But it would be mistaken to think these incidents are isolated or confined only to the hinterlands. Women across the country face criticism for "bold" dressing, endure rude behavior from men in educational institutions, and suffer from eve-teasing and both mental and physical harassment—often at work and sometimes even at home.

What can be done?

Many initiatives have begun to sensitize men—regardless of their economic or social background—to treat women as equals and to respect their intelligence and grace rather than viewing them as the "weaker sex." It is vital to eliminate sexist thoughts, words, and actions. Equality for women is a key pillar on which a truly developed nation stands. Countries like the Nordic states and, to a large extent, China—with a substantially higher percentage of women in senior management roles than India—can serve as inspiring role models.

If by 2047, we aspire to have 40% women in senior management, 30% in leadership positions, and at least 20% as Board Directors and Chairpersons, we will have made tremendous progress towards true equality in India.

We as a nation must progress,
But first, ensure we don't regress.
If we educate our men,
we'll protect our women—
India's sisters deserve more, not less!

Let's try not to deceive,
and correct what we perceive.
In love and inclusion
Lies our true mission—
the joy we give, we will receive!

एक बार धरती और आसमान
लड़ पड़े, कौन महान?
धरती ने कहा मैं सोना उगलती हूँ
सीने में रत्न और फसलें रखती हूँ

आसमान बोला मैं न भेजूं अगर मौसम
तेरी फसलें, रत्न सम्पदा हो जाये ख़तम
बात सही थी दोनों की
छोड़ लड़ाई दोस्ती की

हर कोई भारत देश में भी
अलग है, लेकिन एक जैसा भी
हर कोई चाहता है मौके, काम
किसे नहीं पसंद प्रेम और आराम

सामान अधिकार हैं नर हो या नारी
भेदभाव वाली कुरीतियां खंडित हैं सारी
शिक्षा हो, नौकरी या हो प्रोत्साहन
बराबर का दर्ज़ा और समागम

अपने देश का यही है माहौल अब
लिंग के आधार पर नहीं पक्षपात अब
ये नया भारत है जनाब
यहां बराबरी है, बेनकाब

8.5 Educating the Masses

India is a vast and diverse country, with stark contrasts in prosperity, opportunities, and expectations across its regions. On one hand, we have some of the richest billionaires in the world living in luxurious mansions and high-rise penthouses in cities like Delhi, Mumbai, Bengaluru, Chennai, Hyderabad, and Ahmedabad. On the other hand, millions of poor families struggle daily just to make ends meet, with little room left to dream.

In such a context, expecting every Indian to fully align on important social themes like gender equality, respect for women, and opportunities for LGBTQ+ communities may seem idealistic. Yet, these values are essential for building a society that offers fair and equitable opportunities to all.

Our Founding Father, Mahatma Gandhi, set a powerful example by calling even the lowest castes "Harijans" — Children of God. Over the past decades, we have made significant progress in reducing biases and fostering respect.

To understand the caste system — not to justify it — it originated in times when society needed clear roles to maintain order. Brahmins were priests and teachers, Kshatriyas were warriors and rulers, Vaishyas were merchants and traders, and Sudras were laborers. Dalits, formerly labeled as "untouchables" and later dignified as Harijans, stood outside this hierarchy.

As we strive to become an egalitarian and truly **"viksit"** (developed) nation, we must first clear the cobwebs from our own minds. We need to change not only our thoughts but also our words and actions. Let us educate those around us to avoid derogatory language and embrace everyone as fellow human beings. Together, we can create an environment of love, respect, and inclusion for all.

Don't enter my home, you're not clean,
We used caste and class to be mean.
Through snob and disdain,
we caused hurt and pain,
but it's time to erase this routine.

As we march toward a "viksit" land,
let's recognize each person's stand—
with wit and with dreams,
beyond caste extremes,
helping all rise hand in hand.

ज्ञान का दीप जलाना होगा, हर कोने उजियारा हो
जहाँ विवेक हो भाषा में, और जन चेतना ऊँची हो

वर्ण न हो पहचान किसी की, कर्म ही हो मानक सच्चा,
नव भारत की इस संकल्पना में, सभी को मिले ऊँचा दर्ज़ा

भेद मिटें विचारों के, मन की कुंद सीमाएं टूटें,
सम्मान है हर मानव का हक़, अब तो सब रूढ़ियाँ छूटें

गांधी का वह स्वप्न सजाएँ, जिसमें सबको स्थान मिले,
संवेदना हो, स्पंदन हो, और मानव धर्म का पुष्प खिले

जो अब तक छूटे पथ से, उन्हें साथ चलाना होगा,
विकसित भारत की सच्चाई को सबको ही अपनाना होगा

SECTION 9

Climate Change

9.1 Sustainability

Living and meeting the needs of the present without comprising the planet and the needs of the future generations is the practice of sustainability which is so essential in the world we live in. Over and above living within our means in the present time, sustainability also demands the creation of environments, within homes, organisations and society where humans, other living beings and nature can exist in productive harmony withing an environment that is cleaner, protects the climate and generates lower cost of energy for the planet.

The UN SDGs (Sustainable Development Goals) have been recommended as a call to action for all communities and countries and as nation wanting to have a permanent seat at the high table of global nations, India must encourage all its businesses and social enterprises to optimise asset performance and resource utilization, reduce emissions and build more sustainable global supply chains. There are advantages of adopting sustainability practices early and comprehensively, including saving money, availing of Government incentives and attracting investors who are interested in green entities. This also improves the long-term viability of the enterprise.

It is important that every thinking and well-meaning citizen of the country is also encouraged to adopt and practice sustainability. As a nation, we have come a long way towards adoption of “swacch” practices in every city and village and there is an awareness of energy and food saving which will have long term positive impacts for the country. However, it is important that through green practices and no “greenwashing”, that we continue to make steady and continuous progress towards our sustainability goals as a nation!

There was a time when we were all in haste.
No time to think, no time to taste.
We burnt; we spoilt we were in a hurry.
For the planet we never had any worries
And in the process, we created enormous waste.

But if in this world, we seek to sustain.
The truth before us is very plain.
Conserve we must
And in sustainability we trust
And take actions that Net Zero will attain.

धरती माँ की गोद को स्वच्छ, हरित बनाना है,
भविष्य की पीढ़ियों को, सुंदर जीवन देना है
जरूरतें पूरी हों, पर संसाधन न हो ख़तम,
सस्टेनेबिलिटी का मंत्र, अपनाना है हमदम

ऊर्जा और जल बचाएँ, हरियाली को बढ़ाएं,
कचरा कम से कम हो, प्रकृति को अपनाएं
संघर्ष क्यों? मिल जुल के जीना हमारा सपना,
हर जीव, हर पेड़, ये जीवन सबका है अपना

संयुक्त राष्ट्र के लक्ष्य, हमें राह दिखाते,
हर नागरिक को प्रकृति से सहज ही मिलाते
हरित सोच से आगे बढ़ेगा अगर ये देश हमारा,
सस्टेनेबिलिटी से उज्ज्वल होगा भविष्य सारा!

9.2 Climate Change

In just over a hundred years, the average global temperature has increased by over One Degree Centigrade and is projected to warm by one and half degrees by 2050 and two to four degrees by 2100. This rise if not mitigates could result in one third of the world's population living in Sahara levels climate by 2070 and three billion slowly moving out of areas which will become totally uninhabitable.

The primary culprit for climate change is fossil fuel burning, which has been happening over centuries and releases carbon dioxide and other greenhouse gases into the atmosphere Cabon Dioxide, Methane, Nitrous Oxide and others trap heat in the atmosphere and warm the planet. Deforestation and industrial processes, livestock farming, the use of fertilisers, waste decomposition in landfills and the energy used for air conditioning built spaces, all add to greenhouse gas emissions and the global warming effect. A case in point is the Chotanagpur Plateau in Jharkhand where one of the authors grew up, where the climate was extremely salubrious through the year with the maximum temperature rarely exceeding thirty-five degrees Celsius. Today after excessive deforestation, the summer temperatures can climb to well over forty degrees.

What can we, as responsible citizens do to reduce the alarming effects of our actions in the past and take steps to "sustain and save" in future? It all starts with measurement, and carbon calculations and Sustainability reporting as part of ESG makes us aware of what we are doing. Ensuring that our farms and factories and even our homes and housing colonies adopt sustainability practices, using nonpolluting green technologies including EVs and staying concerned about our environment will keep the planet safe for our future generations.

Through years of waste, we lounged in our seat.
In the energy game, we tried to cheat.
The air, the seas and even the soil
Groaned under all the senseless toil.
Till the planet itself began to feel the heat.

Today we know that every degree we raise.
The temperature of the earth as we burn and raze.
Forests to the ground
And fuels with which we surround.
Will cause us agony and definitely no praise.

धरती की धड़कनें अब तेज़ सुनाई देती हैं
हरियाली के आँचल में तपिश दिखाई देती है
कहने को बस एक डिग्री है, पर असर है बेहिसाब
आने वाले कल में, साँस लेना भी बन जाएगा ख़्वाब

कार्बन के बादल, क्षितिज को ढक चले
पेड़ों के कटने से, खुले आसमान सिमट चले
नदियाँ सूखी हैं, खेतों में पड़ गयी दरारें
लापरवाही मानव की, प्रकृति चीत्कारे

अब भी समय है, जागो, सहेज लो हरियाली,
हर घर, हर खेत में, उगे अब उम्मीद की डाली
सस्टेनेबिलिटी अपनाओ, हर सांस को बचाओ,
आने वाली पीढ़ी के लिए, एक नया सवेरा लाओ

9.3 Sport and Fitness

As countries progress economically, there is sometimes a reverse impact on physical fitness. A state like Gujarat is a case in point where the rich and sweet diets were popular at a time when most women did hard labour in the field and needed the diet to restore their energy. With progress, the percentage of men going into the farms reduced, particularly in the cities but the traditional diet patterns continues leading to corpulence and high incidence of diabetes. As per the World Diabetes Federation, nearly forty million people in India suffer from diabetes with eight to ten percent of the suspected cases from Gujarat.

The problem of poor fitness has been compounded by a long tradition of sport not being sign as livelihood for most youth, particularly men. A young person who loves athletics or swimming or football or hockey often gives up the sport as they enter their college years because of the excessive parental and societal focus on academics. The abysmal performance of India in most international competition including the last Olympics underlines the tragedy that rich don't want to take up sports as a profession and the poor just can't afford it. It's only some middle-class parents in recent years, inspired by many Bollywood tales of sporting heroism, who have encouraged youth to train and compete at the highest levels.

A fit society and one that celebrates excellence in all fields of human endeavour is essential for a nation to progress. The Government is rapidly improving its incentives and its facilities and outstanding support from institutions like Olympic Gold Quest and many corporate funds are creating a platform for sportsmen and women to shine and the obsession for fitness among the young in many cities will hopefully lead to a national desire for fitness!

For many decades we had to get into a scuffle
To test and flex our power of muscle.
We have been perpetually on the run.
with work and play piling up by the ton
No time for fitness in our own life's hustle.

Today we realise we need to stay fit.
Ensure the happiness in our lives stays lit.
Need to find time for sports and games.
and call it balance or other names.
Our health has to be maintained with toil and grit.

माँ ने पूछा, "बेटा, कब खेला था आख़िरी बार?"
बेटा बोला, "माँ, पढ़ाई में ही बीतता है अब हर दिन, बार-बार।"
पिता ने जोड़ा, "हमारे समय में खेलना था रोज़ की बात,
शरीर और मन दोनों को मिलती थी राहत की सौगात।"

बेटा सोचे, "अब ज़िंदगी भागती है तेज़ रफ्तार में,
पर सेहत के बिना तो सब ही फीका है इस संसार में।"
चलना, दौड़ना, खेलना--- यही तो असली जीवन है,
छोटी-छोटी आदतें ही बन जाती बढ़त का दर्पण हैं

माँ ने कहा, "आओ, रोज़ थोड़ा समय खेल को दें,
सिर्फ़ अंक ही नहीं, सेहत में भी आगे बढ़ें।"
पिता बोले, "साथ खेलोगे तो रिश्ते मजबूत होंगे,
स्वस्थ तन-मन से ही तो सपने पूरे होंगे।"

9.4 Respect for all Vocations

Growing up in a small town in Eastern India in the seventies, one of your authors was fascinated by English Language and Literature and his ambition was to study at Cambridge or Oxford in this field. His traditional father advised him that the only way to progress in life would be to take up engineering or medicine, and since he had an aversion for cutting up cockroaches in Biology class, the only option that emerged was Engineering. Of the million plus youth who graduate with engineering degrees every year in India, a vast majority had no particular interest in the subject and just followed the herd with the hope of making into a Tatas or Infosys and getting a good start in life.

The wheel has turned, and it is gratifying that youth from upper middle-class India are choosing to study liberal arts at an Ashoka or Flame University rater than joining rushing towards the IIT JEE or NEET competitive examinations. Beyond the classical blue and grey and rust collar skills that the Industrial Training Institutes are imparting, there are perfectly credible vocations options emerging in mechatronics, dental hygiene, cosmetology, culinary arts, legal work, health sciences, animation, gaming and aviation, to name just a few.

As a nation , we need to create worthwhile jobs for all and with increasing automation and use of AI in manufacturing and information technology, let us ensure that all vocations are seen as equally rewarding and encourage our youth to aspire and compete for opportunities in multiple rewarding and highly respected professions. Into a nation of equal opportunities for all and equal respect for all vocations, our young people should graduate and succeed!

Iqbal the plumber, give me your number.
and here's my friend Hari bringing in some lumber.
Are we rejoicing in our work
that nobody must shirk
And keep no one in deep slumber?

Today we take pride in every vocation.
that helps us to build the nation.
May we celebrate with artists and nurses?
and embrace different folks without any curses.
Let every job receive equal ovation.

प्रत्येक कर्म में निहित है सृजन का दिव्य आलोक,
नहीं किसी व्यवसाय का सीमित या विशिष्ट लोक
माटी को रूप देने वाला, स्वप्नों को रंग प्रदान करता है,
शिल्प हो या विज्ञान, हर एक कर्म जीवन को पूर्ण करता है

सम्मानित हों सभी हस्त, प्रत्येक कौशल का हो आदर,
यही समता का सन्देश, यही मानवता का सच्चा स्वर
रोजगार की विविध दिशाएँ, पर सबका एक ही मान,
सर्व व्यवसाय पूज्य हैं, यही है मानवता का परम ज्ञान

9.5 Dual Intelligence

Since time immemorial, the concept of knowledge and wisdom has been deeply embedded in the Indian psyche. Our Gurus and Rishis were fountains of wisdom, whose profound knowledge was passed down through the Upanishads, the Vedas, and their discourses to disciples – who then spread this wisdom to every corner of the land. Concepts like Vedanta, which introduced the idea of "observed reality," brought existing truths to life in everyday contexts, enriching Indian traditions and culture. Most of us have been nurtured on the vast ocean of this deep knowledge.

In recent times, scientific discoveries such as Niels Bohr's quantum physics, and more recently AI, Generative AI, and Agentic AI, have revisited and often corroborated these ancient insights. The seamless transition from waves to objects, rooted in observed reality, casts Vedantic teachings in a new, contemporary light. The many AI avatars now appearing on our screens—and in our consciousness—are revisiting the fundamentals of data transforming into actionable insights through AI agents, revolutionizing the speed and quality of work.

As the world advances toward Artificial General Intelligence (AGI) and Artificial Super Intelligence (ASI), the smooth flow from data to information, from knowledge to wisdom, will demand abundant *dual intelligence:* AI and machine learning enabling predictive and prescriptive analytics, alongside human intelligence that keeps us ahead of emerging scenarios powered by Generative and Agentic AI solutions. A developed India (Viksit India) will require tremendous growth in thinking, analytical, and synthesis capabilities for its entire people. The future belongs to those who evolve continuously and refuse to remain stagnant.

Did we know when we flew the tech flag high,
And Digital and IoT caught our eye,
That data would bloom to knowledge and more,
Just as we thought wisdom was ours to store—
Along came Agentic AI to shake the sky?

It's Ram who will shine and lead at work,
While Shyam said AI will let me shirk.
Ram embraced it with human insight,
Put his AI to work day and night,
and sped ahead with a confident smirk.

ज्ञान और विज्ञान, दोनों का समुचित मेल हो,
मानव बुद्धि और यंत्र-बुद्धि की एक ही रेल हो
वेदों की गूढ़ बातें, आज तकनीक में झलकती हैं,
सूचना से विवेक तक, कितनी नयी दिशाएँ चमकती हैं

यंत्र-बुद्धि दे समाधान, मानव-बुद्धि दे दृष्टि,
इनके समन्वय से ही बढ़ेगी राष्ट्र की सृष्टि
जो सीखता, बदलता, वही आगे बढ़ता है,
द्वैत बुद्धिमत्ता से ही नव-युग का सृजन होता है

Section 10

Global Bharat

10.1 Increasing Global Respect

India has been a respected member of the global community for centuries. Despite enduring subjugation under Mughal and British rule for several centuries until our independence in 1947, and our proud emergence as a sovereign republic in 1950, we have made remarkable strides over the past decades to become a voice admired and respected across nations.

Many of our leaders have held exalted stature on the world stage — beginning with Mahatma Gandhi, whose unique philosophy of ahimsa and non-violence led India's freedom struggle and eventual liberation. Then there was the scholar and statesman Pandit Jawaharlal Nehru; his forceful and sometimes assertive daughter, Indira Gandhi; the suave and seasoned statesman Atal Bihari Vajpayee; the erudite economist Dr. Manmohan Singh; and in recent times, our widely respected Prime Minister Narendra Modi.

However, a country of India's growing stature cannot afford occasional lapses — spurts of irrational violence, heinous crimes against women that tarnish our image as a safe nation, and dark chapters in history like the Emergency — to overshadow our progress. The persistent challenge of poverty and the sometimes exaggerated perception of India lagging in GDP per capita and Human Development Indices compared to peers also remain obstacles to our narrative of advancement.

What matters most is that every Indian — individual, company, and community alike — takes pride in our origins, our rich history, and the extraordinary capabilities demonstrated by our fellow citizens. The Information Technology services industry, now poised to become a $300 billion global outsourcing leader, alongside global Indian-origin leaders like Indira Nooyi, Satya Nadella, and Sundar Pichai, inspire us all to hold our heads high.

"India," scoffed the cynic, "is but yogis and their rope trick."
Not a nation sleek, polished, or slick.
But our tech might and vision
beyond mere superstition
have forged a reputation both modern and quick.

It's not just the feats of Satya Nadella
or many a young lad and fella
that make us stand tall.
While neighbors may envy all—
our reputation now shines, truly stellar!

भारत की विविधता, संस्कृति की है अपनी शान,
हर रीति, हर पर्व, रचता है एक अलग पहचान
इतिहास के पन्नों में वीरता की अमिट छाप,
नव उपलब्धियों से भी जग में बढ़ा है प्रताप

चंद्रयान से लेकर डिजिटल क्रांति तक,
हर क्षेत्र में भारत का है अद्भुत उत्कर्ष
वैज्ञानिक शोध, नवाचार की मिसाल
विश्व मंच पर चमकता भारत का भव्य भाल

विदेशों में भी गूंजती है भारतीयता की बात,
संस्कृति, योग, आयुर्वेद का बढ़ता सम्मान साथ
हर भारतीय का गर्व, अब सीमाओं से पार है
विश्व समुदाय में भी भारत का सम्मान अपार है

एकजुट होकर, राष्ट्र गौरव को करें और प्रबल,
विश्व मंच पर लहराएँ, भारत का ध्वज अचल
स्वाभिमान, एकता, प्रगति का यह संगम,
राष्ट्र गौरव की यह भावना, फैले जग में हरदम

10.2 Role of Media

Media has always played—and continues to play—a pivotal role in shaping the perception of our country and its leaders. Be it in politics, literature, or business, the image of India and its icons is significantly built and amplified by the media. As authors deeply in love with and concerned for our nation, we have often been moved by the power of exceptional reporting—from the golden days of All India Radio and Doordarshan to the consistent contributions of national dailies like *The Times of India, The Indian Express, Dainik Bhaskar, and The Hindu.*

In recent years, dynamic news anchors like Rajdeep Sardesai, Arnab Goswami, Ravish Kumar, and Barkha Dutt have created waves—winning both admiration and criticism—from casual viewers and serious news aficionados alike. Today, however, the biggest draw is social media, where many of us first encounter breaking stories through our Linked In or X (formerly twitter) feeds.

Influencers now play a powerful role in curating what we see—often framing news not as we ought to see it, but as they want us to. Whether branded "Godi Media" or accused of bias from across the political spectrum, the reality is inescapable: media has infiltrated every corner of our consciousness and become an inseparable part of our lives.

So how do we respond in this flood of information and propaganda that bombards our senses every waking moment? The wisest path is not to leap to conclusions. Instead, seek out a range of credible, even opposing viewpoints before forming your own. Building a well-informed opinion is a responsibility—and a right—we owe ourselves. When we contribute our own rational voices to the public discourse, we serve both ourselves and our country.

Too often we're stuck with the Press,
whose coverage can leave us in distress.
Can we have news sans all the noise,
without another shouting voice—
that aims more to impress than express?

The media's true role, when it's right,
is to spark both ideas and insight.
Praise where it's due, expose what's unfair—
Hold every power to public glare.
Only then will India shine bright!

मीडिया है समाज का आईना, दिखाता हर रंग हमें
राजनीति, साहित्य, व्यापार -- हर क्षेत्र में संग है ये

कभी रेडियो, कभी अख़बार, कभी टीवी की बात,
सोशल मीडिया से मिलती है हर खबर की सौगात

सूचनाओं की बाढ़ में, सच-झूठ का फर्क मिट रहा
हर विचार, हर खबर, एक छलावा है रच रहा

मीडिया प्रभावित करता है सोच को, राय बन रही है
कभी निष्पक्ष, कभी पक्षपाती, दोनों तरफ ही ढल रही है

मीडिया, तुम हर घटना को समझो, सोचो, फिर खबर बनाओ,
लेने दो अपने निर्णय दर्शक को, विविध दृष्टिकोण दिखाओ

गोडी मीडिया या निष्पक्षता की पुकार,
हर नागरिक को चाहिए विवेक का आधार

सूचना का युग है तो जिम्मेदारी भी हम सबकी है
सजग हों, अच्छा कंटेंट मांगें, इसी में होशियारी है

10.3 Indian Diaspora Participation

Many decades ago, the first traders ventured to Dubai, and aspiring engineers started applying for Master's degrees in Computer Science in the USA. Many stayed back to build their careers, acquire green cards, and eventually become citizens — not just in the US, but also in the UK, Europe, Australia, Singapore, Bahrain, Durban, and other global hubs. From a trickle, the Indian diaspora swelled from a few hundred to thousands, and today, to several millions.

The Indian diaspora — what our friend MR Rangaswami calls his Indiaspora group — includes thought leaders and policymakers across various countries, especially the USA. Owing to their strong academic foundations in India, many have a natural inclination to contribute — not just through remittances, but also through ideas, entrepreneurship, and social investments back home.

While some do tend to preach without a full grasp of India's ground realities, mature and mission-driven communities such as Indiaspora, the Pan-IIT group, and the WHEELS India network are making meaningful contributions through conferences, innovative solutions, and philanthropic investments.

Today, the diaspora is a powerful and influential community — and rightfully so. Every year, they are recognized on a national stage during Pravasi Bharatiya Divas. Our Prime Minister and other top leaders make it a point to engage with diaspora communities during foreign visits, and also offer an audience to diaspora leaders when they return to India.

As responsible citizens, we must welcome their engagement, take their criticisms with a pinch of salt, and embrace their ideas — especially when they contribute to the nation's progress.

There were tales of NRIs in dismay,
who flew in each December to have their say.
They'd criticize with flair,
and then vanish in the air –
while locals just sighed in dismay.

But now, with millions calling India their own,
the diaspora's influence has fully grown.
They invest, they advise,
they help India rise –
so let's give them their well-earned throne!

कभी गाँव की गलियों में, खेलते थे छोटे सपने,
धीरे-धीरे बढ़े कदम, पहुँचे महानगरों में अपने
मुंबई की भीड़ से निकले, कुछ सपनों के परवाने,
विदेशों की ओर बढ़े, नए क्षितिज को पाने

दुबई की रेत हो या न्यूयॉर्क की रौशनी,
हर जगह बसता है भारत, अमिट संस्कृति की निशानी
इंजीनियर, डॉक्टर, व्यापारी या वैज्ञानिक,
हर क्षेत्र में चमके भारतीय, बने विश्व में विशिष्ट

कुछ भेजते हैं धन, कुछ पहुंचा देते हैं विचार,
देश की प्रगति में, निभाते हैं अपना किरदार
कभी सम्मेलन, कभी निवेश, कभी मिलन परिवार का
हर मंच पर बढ़ाते गौरव, ऊँचा करते भाल भारत माँ का

प्रवासी दिवस पर मिलती है पहचान
नेताओं से मान, भावनाओं का सम्मान
कभी आलोचना, कोई सुझाव, कभी सलाह
हर भाव में छुपी है भारत की प्रगति की चाह

देश से दूर रहकर भी, दिल है यहीं कहीं,
हर उपलब्धि में गूंजती है देशप्रेम की धुन वहीं
अतुलित है प्रवासियों का योगदान,
उनकी ऊर्जा से बने भारत और भी महान

10.4 Building National Pride

During a discussion at the renowned Harvard Business School, one of our authors recalled a memorable remark made by his batch mate, Mark Brown:

"We Americans may argue and disagree on domestic or political issues, but when faced with an external threat, we set aside our internal differences and unite as one nation."

This powerful sentiment was evident in the aftermath of the World Trade Center attacks, showcasing the kind of unwavering national unity that defines great nations. Such expressions of nationalism aren't exclusive to the United States—we have seen similar unifying moments in countries like China, Russia, the UAE, and Singapore.

India, too, has witnessed such collective pride—be it during the 1971 Bangladesh Liberation War or through historic moments in sports, like Kapil Dev's 1983 and Dhoni's 2011 Cricket World Cup victories. These instances brought the entire country together in joyful celebration and patriotic unity. What we need now are more such opportunities to connect, collaborate, and come together as one nation.

However, it is crucial to distinguish **nationalism** from **political ideology.** Supporting or opposing a political leader does not define one's patriotism. True national fervour—just as Mark Brown highlighted—is **nonpartisan, apolitical, and unbiased.** It stems from a genuine sense of pride and responsibility, inspiring us to transcend personal differences and unite in our collective identity as Indians.

If we can embrace this spirit on our journey toward **Viksit Bharat** (Developed India), we can truly live up to Swami Vivekananda's timeless call:
"Arise, Awake, and Stop Not till the Goal is Reached!"

Sisters and Brothers of America, he said,
to Chicago's Parliament, with dignity widespread.
When we hear Vivekananda, the sage,
His grace and resolve leap off the page—
We're proud of this land where knowledge is widespread!

Through decades, our history has brightly turned page,
Indian IT now has a new global image.
With reasons so many for patriotic pride,
we stride together, shoulder to side,
As India rises with confidence on the world stage !

Rumi

राष्ट्र का गौरव है हमारी असली पहचान,
एकता और प्रेम से बनता है इसका सम्मान
राजनीति से ऊपर उठकर, जुड़ें देश के नाम,
संकट में साथ आना, यही है सच्चा काम

क्रिकेट की जीत हो या युद्ध का मैदान
हर घडी में सर्वोच्च है भारत की एकता महान
गर्व और जिम्मेदारी का भाव जब मन में आए
देशहित में हर मतभेद खुद-ब-खुद मिट जाए

स्वामी विवेकानंद की वाणी हमें दिखाए राह,
"उठो, जागो, रुको मत"--- यही है सच्ची चाह
मिलकर संकल्प लेना होगा, बनाएं भारत को महान,
राष्ट्र गौरव की भावना हो जागृत, उपजे देश के लिए सम्मान

Conclusion

Making Visit Bharat Happen

The themes we have explored in this book aim to reflect the multifaceted journey of a nation that has shown commendable progress in some areas, while falling short in others. Through a blend of prose, limericks, and poetry, we've attempted to shed light on key issues, celebrate achievements, and chart a path forward.

Together, we've traversed through India's evolving vision—its historical roots, its strides in strengthening physical and digital infrastructure, and its uneven economic trajectory. We've examined the machinery of administration over seventy-five years of independence, the rise of a new entrepreneurial era, the focus on people-centric development, and the call for love and inclusion in society. We've also looked at the emerging imperatives of a Global Bharat—rooted in strong fundamentals and ready for a rightful place at the global high table.

As we reflect on the journey of our nation—its past, present, and future, three key themes emerge that merit re-emphasis:

First, we can take immense pride in the progress we've made. From centuries of resilience leading up to independence, through the last seven decades, and particularly in the past twenty years of economic liberalization, India has demonstrated remarkable tenacity and growth.

Second, some early policy choices—especially the adoption of a socialistic, large-government model—may have delayed our economic momentum. While other Asian economies surged ahead, India missed the bus in matching their pace of development, particularly visible in the stories of China, Vietnam, and the so-called Asian Tigers.

Third, although India has emerged as a global leader in services—especially in technology and outsourcing—we still have significant ground to cover in manufacturing, agriculture, and product innovation. These sectors remain key to creating a truly self-reliant and prosperous nation.

Viksit India is not just a dream—it is a possibility within our grasp. To realise it, we must adopt a model of accelerated, inclusive growth that sustains an 8% consumption-led GDP increase for the next two decades. This will not only elevate our overall GDP but also enhance our GDP per capita, ensuring prosperity for every Indian.

India's Nobel laureate, Rabindranath Tagore, envisioned a nation where:

"The mind is without fear and the head is held high...
Where knowledge is free...
Where the mind is led forward by thee into ever-widening thought and action—
into that heaven of freedom, my Father, let my country awake."

No one could have expressed this aspiration more beautifully. It remains the collective hope of every Indian who dreams of a better, stronger, more inclusive nation.

If this book has encouraged you to dream a little bigger, think a little deeper, and act a little bolder for the future of India—then we have truly fulfilled our purpose.